GOODSON MUMBA

# Banking Reinvented

*Disruption and Transformation in Finance*

*Copyright © 2024 by Goodson Mumba*

*All rights reserved. No part of this publication may be reproduced, stored or transmitted in any form or by any means, electronic, mechanical, photocopying, recording, scanning, or otherwise without written permission from the publisher. It is illegal to copy this book, post it to a website, or distribute it by any other means without permission.*

*First edition*

*ISBN: 9798333952318*

*This book was professionally typeset on Reedsy. Find out more at reedsy.com*

# Contents

| | | |
|---|---|---|
| *Preface* | | ix |
| *Acknowledgments* | | xii |
| *Dedication* | | xiii |
| *Disclaimer* | | xiv |
| 1 | Chapter 1: The Evolution of Banking | 1 |
| | 1.1: The Origins of Banking | 1 |
| | 1.2: Traditional Banking Models | 3 |
| | 1.3: Early Disruptions in Banking | 6 |
| | 1.4: The Rise of Digital Banking | 9 |
| | 1.5: Regulatory Challenges and Responses | 11 |
| | 1.6: Case Studies: Legacy Banks vs. Challenger Banks | 14 |
| 2 | Chapter 2: Fintech Revolution: Shaping the Future of Finance | 18 |
| | 2.1: Introduction to Fintech | 18 |
| | 2.2: Fintech Innovations in Payments | 20 |
| | 2.3: Peer-to-Peer Lending Platforms | 22 |
| | 2.4: Robo-Advisors and Wealth Management | 25 |
| | 2.5: Blockchain and Cryptocurrencies | 27 |
| | 2.6: The Impact of Fintech on Traditional Banking Models | 29 |
| 3 | Chapter 3: Digital Transformation in Banking | 32 |
| | 3.1: The Shift to Digital Channels | 32 |

3.2: The Banking Apps: Convenience vs. Security — 34
3.3: Artificial Intelligence in Banking Operations — 37
3.4: Big Data and Analytics in Banking — 39
3.5: Personalization and Customer Experience — 41
3.6: Cybersecurity Challenges in the Digital Era — 43

4 Chapter 4: Open Banking and API Economy — 46
4.1: Understanding Open Banking — 46
4.2: The Role of APIs in Banking — 49
4.3: Benefits for Consumers and Businesses — 51
4.4: Challenges and Risks of Open Banking — 54
4.5: Global Perspectives on Open Banking — 58
4.6: Future Trends and Opportunities — 60

5 Chapter 5: The Rise of Neobanks and Challenger Banks — 63
5.1: Defining Neobanks and Challenger Banks — 63
5.2: Disrupting the Status Quo: Neobanks vs. Traditional Banks — 65
5.3: Business Models and Revenue Streams — 67
5.4: Neobanks Around the World: Case Studies — 69
5.5: Partnerships and Collaborations with Neobanks — 71
5.6: Regulatory Considerations for Neobanks — 73

6 Chapter 6: AI and Automation in Banking Operations — 75
6.1: AI Applications in Banking — 75
6.2: Chatbots and Virtual Assistants — 77
6.3: Risk Management and Fraud Detection — 79
6.4: Process Automation and Efficiency Gains — 80
6.5 Challenges of AI Implementation in Banking — 82

|     |     |
| --- | --- |
| 6.6: Ethical Considerations and Future Outlook | 86 |
| 7 Chapter 7: Financial Inclusion and Access | 89 |
| 7.1: The Importance of Financial Inclusion | 89 |
| 7.2: Technology Solutions for Financial Inclusion | 91 |
| 7.3: Banking the Unbanked: Initiatives and Challenges | 92 |
| 7.4: Microfinance and Alternative Banking Models | 94 |
| 7.5: Partnerships for Inclusive Banking | 96 |
| 7.6: Measuring Success: Impact Metrics and Case Studies | 98 |
| 8 Chapter 8: Sustainability and Responsible Banking | 100 |
| 8.1: The Role of Banks in Sustainable Development | 100 |
| 8.2: Environmental, Social, and Governance (ESG) Criteria | 102 |
| 8.3: Green Finance and Climate Action | 104 |
| 8.4: Social Impact Investing and Community Development | 105 |
| 8.5: Challenges and Opportunities for Responsible Banking | 107 |
| 8.6: Leading the Change: Best Practices in Responsible Banking | 109 |
| 9 Chapter 9: RegTech and Compliance Innovation | 114 |
| 9.1: Introduction to Regulatory Technology (RegTech) | 114 |
| 9.2: Compliance Challenges in Banking | 116 |
| 9.3: Automated Compliance Solutions | 118 |
| 9.4: Regulators' Perspectives on RegTech | 120 |
| 9.5: Adoption Strategies for RegTech Solutions | 121 |
| 9.6: Future Trends in Compliance and Regulation | 123 |

- 10 Chapter 10: The Future of Money: Cryptocurrencies and...   126
  - 10.1: Understanding Cryptocurrencies   126
  - 10.2: Bitcoin and Beyond: Altcoins and Tokens   128
  - 10.3: Challenges and Opportunities of Cryptocurrency Adoption   130
  - 10.4: Central Bank Digital Currencies (CBDCs): Concept and Implementation   132
  - 10.5: The Role of CBDCs in Financial Systems   134
  - 10.6: Implications for Traditional Banking and Monetary Policy   136
- 11 Chapter 11: Biometric Authentication and Security   138
  - 11.1: The Need for Stronger Authentication Methods   138
  - 11.2: Biometric Technologies in Banking   140
  - 11.3: Advantages and Limitations of Biometric Authentication   142
  - 11.4: Addressing Privacy Concerns   144
  - 11.5: Biometric Security in Mobile Banking   146
  - 11.6: Future Development in Biometric Authentication   148
- 12 Chapter 12: Wealth Management in the Digital Age   150
  - 12.1: The Changing Landscape of Wealth Management   150
  - 12.2: Robo-Advisors vs. Traditional Financial Advisors   152
  - 12.3: Personalized Investment Strategies   154
  - 12.4: Digital Tools for Portfolio Management   156

|    |    |
|---|---|
| 12.5: Challenges and Risks in Digital Wealth Management | 158 |
| 12.6: Hybrid Models: Blending Human Expertise with Technology | 160 |
| 13 Chapter 13: Cybersecurity in Banking | 163 |
| 13.1: The Growing Threat Landscape | 163 |
| 13.2: Common Cyber Attacks in Banking | 165 |
| 13.3: Building a Robust Cybersecurity Framework | 167 |
| 13.4: Incident Response and Crisis Management | 169 |
| 13.5: Cybersecurity Awareness and Training | 171 |
| 13.6: Collaborative Approaches to Cyber Defense | 172 |
| 14 Chapter 14: Data Privacy and Consumer Protection | 175 |
| 14.1: The Importance of Data Privacy in Banking | 175 |
| 14.2: Regulatory Landscape: GDPR, CCPA, and Beyond | 177 |
| 14.3: Data Governance and Compliance | 180 |
| 14.4: Transparency and Consent Management | 183 |
| 14.5: Building Trust Through Privacy and Security | 186 |
| 14.6: Emerging Trends in Data Privacy Regulation | 189 |
| 15 Chapter 15: The Road Ahead: Navigating Uncertainty and... | 191 |
| 15.1: Reflections on the Banking Evolution | 191 |
| 15.2: Anticipating Future Disruptions | 193 |
| 15.3: Strategies for Innovation and Adaptation | 194 |
| 15.4: Investing in Talent and Culture Change | 196 |
| 15.5: Collaboration and Ecosystem Building | 197 |
| 15.6: Charting a Course for Success in the New Era of Banking | 198 |

*About the Author* 200

# Preface

In the dynamic world of finance, change is the only constant. From the earliest days of barter systems to the rise of sophisticated financial instruments, banking has evolved in ways that have fundamentally reshaped economies and societies. Today, we stand at the precipice of yet another transformation – one driven by technological innovation, shifting consumer expectations, and an increasingly interconnected global economy.

"Banking Reinvented: Disruption and Transformation in Finance" is a comprehensive exploration of this ongoing revolution. This book delves into the seismic shifts that are redefining the financial landscape, from the rise of fintech and digital currencies to the advent of artificial intelligence and blockchain technology. It examines the challenges and opportunities that arise from these changes, offering insights into how traditional banks can adapt and thrive in this new era.

The narrative is anchored by the journey of our protagonist, Michael, whose experiences and insights provide a human perspective on the complexities of the financial industry. Through his eyes, we explore the historical context of banking, the pivotal moments of disruption, and the innovative strategies that are shaping the future of finance.

This book is structured into fifteen chapters, each focusing on a critical aspect of the banking transformation. We begin with the evolution of banking, tracing its origins and examining the traditional models that have dominated the industry for centuries. We then transition to the rise of digital banking, exploring the fintech revolution and the profound impact of technological advancements on payment systems, lending platforms, and wealth management.

As we move forward, we delve into the intricacies of digital transformation, from the shift to digital channels and the role of artificial intelligence to the critical importance of cybersecurity and data privacy. We examine the rise of neobanks and challenger banks, highlighting their disruptive potential and the regulatory challenges they face. The chapters on financial inclusion and responsible banking underscore the need for a more inclusive and sustainable financial system, while the discussions on RegTech and the future of money explore the innovative solutions that are emerging to address regulatory and monetary challenges.

The final chapters focus on the road ahead, offering strategies for navigating uncertainty, embracing innovation, and charting a course for success in the new era of banking. These insights are not only relevant for industry professionals but also for anyone interested in understanding the forces shaping the future of finance.

"Banking Reinvented" is more than just a chronicle of change; it is a call to action. It urges readers to embrace the opportunities presented by this transformation, to innovate fearlessly, and to lead with vision and purpose. As we navigate the complexities of the modern financial landscape, this book serves as a guide, providing the knowledge and inspiration needed to thrive in an era of unprecedented disruption.

I invite you to join Michael on this journey, to explore the fascinating world of banking, and to discover the limitless possibilities that lie ahead.

Welcome to the future of finance.

Sincerely,

Goodson Mumba

# Acknowledgments

I would like to eternally and gratefully acknowledge the Almighty God for the infinite intelligence from His universal mind where we draw from all that we come to know and are yet to know. May I also acknowledge and thank everyone that has played a part in my journey of life in terms of spiritual, moral, emotional and material support.

# Dedication

I extend my sincerest gratitude to my beloved wife, Edith Mumba, and our children, Angelina, Lubuto, Letticia, Lulumbi, and Butusho, for their unwavering support and understanding throughout the conception, writing, and eventual publication of this book, despite the sacrifices and challenges they endured.

# Disclaimer

This book is a work of fiction. Names, characters, businesses, places, events, and incidents are either the products of the author's imagination or used in a fictitious manner. Any resemblance to actual persons, living or dead, or actual events is purely coincidental.

# 1

# Chapter 1: The Evolution of Banking

## 1.1: The Origins of Banking

Michael Sawyer stood at the entrance of the British Museum, clutching a notebook filled with scribbled ideas and questions. His curiosity about the origins of banking had brought him here, seeking a deeper understanding of the system he had worked within for decades.

Inside, Michael was greeted by Dr. Eleanor Price, a renowned historian specializing in ancient finance. She led him through the echoing halls to a dimly lit room filled with artifacts from ancient Mesopotamia.

"Welcome, Michael," Dr. Price began, gesturing to a display of clay tablets. "This is where it all started, over 4,000 years ago. These tablets are records of the first known banking activities."

Michael leaned in, examining the cuneiform inscriptions. "What exactly are these?" he asked, his voice tinged with awe.

"These are loan agreements," Dr. Price explained. "The people of Mesopotamia used these tablets to record transactions.

Temples and palaces acted as proto-banks, where grain and other commodities were deposited and loans were given out."

As they moved to the next exhibit, Michael learned about the role of these early banks in facilitating trade and managing resources. Dr. Price's descriptions painted a vivid picture of bustling markets and the vital role of banking in enabling commerce.

"But how did we move from these early systems to the structured banking models we know today?" Michael inquired, eager to connect the dots.

Dr. Price smiled. "It was a gradual evolution. Let me show you something." She led him to a section displaying ancient Greek and Roman artifacts. "By the time of the Greeks and Romans, banking had become more sophisticated. Money changers, or trapezitai, offered loans, accepted deposits, and facilitated currency exchange."

Michael was captivated by the stories of ancient bankers like Pasion, a former slave who became one of the wealthiest bankers in Athens. The transition from barter to coinage had revolutionized trade, making banking services more critical than ever.

Their journey continued through the Middle Ages, where Michael learned about the rise of merchant banks in medieval Italy. Dr. Price explained how families like the Medici had transformed banking by introducing double-entry bookkeeping and establishing branches across Europe.

"These innovations laid the groundwork for modern banking," she said. "But it wasn't until the establishment of the Bank of England in 1694 that we saw the birth of the central banking system as we know it."

Michael's eyes widened as he listened to the tale of William

Paterson and the founding of the Bank of England. The bank had been created to manage government debt and stabilize the economy, a model that would be emulated worldwide.

As they concluded their tour, Dr. Price summarized, "Banking has always been about trust, innovation, and adapting to the needs of society. Understanding its origins helps us appreciate the transformations we're witnessing today."

Michael thanked Dr. Price, his mind buzzing with newfound insights. The origins of banking were more intricate and fascinating than he had ever imagined. As he stepped out of the museum, he felt a renewed sense of purpose. His journey to reinvent banking was rooted in a rich history of innovation and adaptation.

He was ready to explore how these ancient principles could inspire the future of finance.

## 1.2: Traditional Banking Models

Michael Sawyer left the British Museum with a newfound appreciation for the ancient origins of banking. He was eager to understand how these early systems had evolved into the traditional banking models he had worked within for so many years. His next destination was the London headquarters of Sterling & Co., one of the oldest and most respected banks in the world.

Inside the grand building, he was met by Edward Collins, the bank's chief historian. Edward, a distinguished man with a wealth of knowledge and a passion for banking history, led Michael through a corridor adorned with portraits of past chairmen and original documents from the bank's founding days.

"Our story begins in 1725," Edward began as they entered a room filled with artifacts from the bank's early years. "Sterling & Co. started as a small family business offering loans and safekeeping services. Our founders recognized the need for a trusted intermediary to manage financial transactions."

Michael examined a beautifully preserved ledger. "This must have been quite an innovation at the time," he remarked.

"Indeed," Edward replied. "In those days, banking was about providing a safe place for merchants to deposit their money and facilitating trade through loans. The model was built on trust and reputation. The more reliable the bank, the more customers it attracted."

As they moved through the exhibits, Edward explained how Sterling & Co. expanded its services over the centuries. By the 19th century, the bank had introduced savings accounts, offering interest to depositors, and had begun issuing banknotes, which became a precursor to modern currency.

"This period was crucial," Edward said. "Banks started playing a vital role in the economy, not just as safe keepers but as institutions that could lend money to businesses and individuals, driving economic growth."

Michael was particularly intrigued by the stories of the industrial era, where banks like Sterling & Co. financed infrastructure projects such as railways and factories. This era marked the emergence of commercial banking, where banks became engines of economic development, providing the capital needed for large-scale industrial ventures.

"However," Edward continued, "with growth came regulation. The Bank Charter Act of 1844, for example, was significant. It gave the Bank of England the sole right to issue banknotes, which helped stabilize the currency and prevent bank failures."

They paused before a display featuring an array of historical banknotes and checks. "Regulation has always been a double-edged sword," Michael mused. "It stabilizes the system but also imposes constraints that can stifle innovation."

Edward nodded. "True. And that balance between innovation and regulation is something banks have navigated for centuries. By the 20th century, traditional banks were not just about deposits and loans. They had expanded into investment banking, offering services like underwriting, mergers and acquisitions, and wealth management."

Michael listened intently as Edward described the post-World War II banking boom. This era saw the rise of global banking giants, facilitated by advancements in technology and communication. Traditional banking models now encompassed a wide range of financial services, all designed to meet the diverse needs of their clients.

"Our model remained fundamentally the same until the late 20th century," Edward said, leading Michael to a modern section of the exhibit. "Then came the digital revolution, which set the stage for the disruptions we see today."

Reflecting on the tour, Michael realized how the core principles of trust, service diversification, and regulation had shaped traditional banking models. But he also saw the limitations of these models in a rapidly changing world. The rigid structures and slow pace of innovation were not suited for the digital age, where speed, convenience, and customer-centric services were paramount.

As he left Sterling & Co., Michael felt a deepened resolve. He had seen the evolution from ancient practices to traditional banking models and now understood the historical context of the challenges and opportunities facing the industry. His journey to reinvent banking was not just about embracing the new but also about honoring and learning from the past.

Next, he would delve into the fintech revolution, where he hoped to find the answers and inspiration needed to truly transform finance for the modern era.

## 1.3: Early Disruptions in Banking

Michael Sawyer's exploration of banking history continued to the archives of the Royal Bank of Scotland (RBS), housed in a stately building that exuded centuries of financial tradition. His guide this time was Clara Hughes, an energetic historian with a passion for the pivotal moments that shaped modern banking.

"Michael, welcome to our archives," Clara greeted him warmly. "Today, we'll explore some of the early disruptions that shook the banking world and set the stage for modern innovations."

They began in a room filled with artifacts from the 18th century. Clara pointed to a document framed on the wall. "This is one of the first banknotes issued by the RBS in 1727. The introduction of paper money was a revolutionary step away from coin-based currency."

Michael nodded, recalling his recent learnings. "I imagine that wasn't received well by everyone at the time."

"Absolutely," Clara confirmed. "Many were skeptical, but the convenience and security of paper money eventually won them over. This was one of the earliest disruptions, shifting how people perceived and used money."

They moved to another exhibit featuring the Industrial

Revolution. Clara explained how banks like RBS began financing massive infrastructure projects. "Railways, factories, and new technologies needed substantial capital, which traditional banking models had to adapt to provide."

"These investments must have transformed the economy," Michael commented, imagining the bustling scenes of construction and innovation.

"Indeed. But let's talk about a more controversial disruption: the advent of joint-stock banking," Clara said, leading him to a section dedicated to the 19th century. "Before this, banks were mostly partnerships, which limited their growth. Joint-stock banks allowed for more shareholders, which meant more capital and expansion."

Michael studied a ledger from one of the first joint-stock banks. "This must have democratized banking to some extent, making it accessible to more people."

"Yes, it did, but it also introduced new risks," Clara replied. "The infamous Overend, Gurney & Co. collapse in 1866 highlighted the dangers of speculation and poor management. It caused a banking panic, leading to reforms that emphasized the need for regulatory oversight."

They paused before a display of telegraphs and early computing machines. Clara smiled. "Another game-changer was the telegraph and later, computers. These technologies drastically sped up communication and transactions, making global banking a reality."

Michael marveled at an old telegraph machine. "I can't imagine banking without the instant communication we take for granted today."

Clara nodded. "Each technological advancement disrupted the existing system, forcing banks to adapt. And it wasn't just technology. Policy changes, like the establishment of the Federal Reserve in 1913, centralized banking in the United States and introduced a lender of last resort to prevent bank runs."

They discussed the Great Depression and the subsequent New Deal reforms. "The Glass-Steagall Act of 1933 was another major disruption," Clara explained. "It separated commercial and investment banking, aiming to curb the kind of speculative risks that led to the 1929 crash."

Michael felt a growing appreciation for how crises often spurred significant changes in banking. "It seems like every disruption, whether technological or regulatory, pushed banks to evolve and innovate."

"Exactly," Clara said. "The lesson here is that disruption is a catalyst for progress. Each challenge forced the industry to rethink and rebuild, often leading to stronger, more resilient systems."

As they concluded their tour, Clara left Michael with a parting thought. "Understanding these early disruptions helps us see patterns. The challenges you're facing today with fintech and digital banking aren't new; they're part of a long history of innovation and adaptation."

Michael left the archives with a deeper understanding of the cyclical nature of disruption in banking. Each innovation and crisis had pushed the industry forward, paving the way for the next leap. Equipped with this knowledge, he felt more prepared to navigate the modern disruptions he was studying.

His next stop would delve into the rise of digital banking, where he hoped to uncover the latest wave of innovation transforming the financial landscape.

## 1.4: The Rise of Digital Banking

Michael Sawyer found himself in the heart of Silicon Valley, where the spirit of innovation was palpable. He had arranged to meet with an old friend and former colleague, Rachel Lin, now a leading figure in the world of digital banking. Rachel had left the traditional banking sector years ago to join one of the first digital-only banks, pioneering a transformation that Michael was eager to understand.

Rachel greeted Michael in the lobby of a sleek, modern building that housed her company's headquarters. The open floor plan, with its glass walls and buzzing activity, contrasted sharply with the grand, historic halls of the traditional banks Michael had recently visited.

"Welcome to the future, Michael," Rachel said with a smile, leading him to a conference room equipped with state-of-the-art technology. "Let's talk about how digital banking came to be."

As they settled in, Rachel began recounting the early days of digital banking. "It all started in the late 1990s with the rise of the internet. Banks began offering online services, allowing customers to check balances, transfer money, and pay bills from their computers."

Michael nodded, remembering the cautious optimism of those early days. "I recall the skepticism from many of our colleagues. They couldn't imagine banking without physical branches."

Rachel laughed. "True, but customers quickly embraced the convenience. By the early 2000s, internet banking had become mainstream, and banks that were slow to adopt it found themselves struggling to keep up."

She explained how digital banking evolved further with the advent of smartphones. "The launch of the iPhone in 2007 was a game-changer. Mobile banking apps became essential, offering even more convenience. Customers could now manage their finances on the go, leading to an explosion in demand for digital services."

Michael listened intently as Rachel described the technological innovations that followed. "We saw the rise of user-friendly interfaces, real-time notifications, and enhanced security features like biometric authentication. Banks began investing heavily in technology to stay competitive."

Rachel shared stories of her own experiences at the digital bank. "We were able to offer services traditional banks couldn't match. Without the overhead of physical branches, we could provide better interest rates and lower fees. Our focus was entirely on the customer experience, using data analytics to personalize services and predict customer needs."

Michael was particularly fascinated by the impact of big data and artificial intelligence. "How did AI change the game for you?" he asked.

"AI allowed us to automate many processes, from customer service chatbots to fraud detection systems," Rachel explained. "It also enabled us to offer personalized financial advice, tailoring recommendations based on individual spending habits and financial goals."

They discussed the challenges, too. "Cybersecurity has always been a major concern," Rachel admitted. "As we became more digital, the threats evolved. We had to invest heavily in security measures to protect our customers' data and build their trust."

Michael appreciated the candid insights. "It seems like

digital banking required a complete cultural shift, not just technological upgrades."

"Absolutely," Rachel agreed. "We had to foster an environment of continuous innovation, agility, and customer-centric thinking. It wasn't enough to just digitize existing services; we had to rethink banking from the ground up."

As their conversation drew to a close, Rachel emphasized the ongoing nature of the digital banking revolution. "We're just at the beginning. The possibilities with technologies like blockchain, open banking, and further advancements in AI are immense. The future of banking will be more interconnected, intelligent, and seamless than we can even imagine today."

Michael left Silicon Valley with a renewed sense of excitement and purpose. The rise of digital banking had not only transformed the industry but also set the stage for even greater innovations. He realized that embracing these changes was essential for the future of finance.

Next, Michael planned to delve into the regulatory challenges and responses that had shaped the landscape of digital banking, hoping to gain a comprehensive understanding of how to navigate and thrive in this dynamic environment.

## 1.5: Regulatory Challenges and Responses

Michael Sawyer's next destination was Washington, D.C., where he had scheduled a meeting with Jonathan Mitchell, a seasoned financial regulator who had witnessed firsthand the evolution of banking regulations. Jonathan, now a consultant, had agreed to share his insights into the regulatory challenges that had accompanied the rise of digital banking.

Michael arrived at Jonathan's office, located in a historic

building not far from the Capitol. Jonathan, a tall man with a stern yet approachable demeanor, greeted him warmly and led him to a conference room filled with stacks of documents and reports.

"Welcome, Michael," Jonathan said, offering him a seat. "Let's dive into the regulatory landscape that has shaped modern banking, especially in the digital age."

Michael was eager to understand how regulations had evolved alongside the rapid technological advancements. Jonathan began with the early regulatory frameworks that had governed traditional banking. "In the early days, regulations were fairly straightforward, focusing on ensuring liquidity and preventing fraud. But as banks grew and diversified, so did the regulatory requirements."

Jonathan pointed to a timeline on the wall, marking significant regulatory milestones. "The 1980s and 1990s saw a wave of deregulation, which encouraged innovation but also led to increased risk-taking. This culminated in the financial crisis of 2008, a pivotal moment that reshaped the entire regulatory landscape."

Michael nodded, recalling the chaos and uncertainty of that time. "I remember the panic. It felt like the entire system was on the brink of collapse."

"Exactly," Jonathan agreed. "The crisis exposed significant weaknesses in the regulatory framework. In response, governments around the world introduced sweeping reforms. In the United States, we saw the introduction of the Dodd-Frank Act in 2010, which aimed to reduce risks and increase transparency."

Jonathan highlighted key provisions of Dodd-Frank, such as the establishment of the Consumer Financial Protection

Bureau (CFPB) and stricter capital requirements for banks. "These measures were designed to prevent a repeat of the crisis by increasing oversight and accountability."

As the discussion turned to digital banking, Jonathan explained the unique regulatory challenges it presented. "Digital banking brought new risks, especially in terms of cybersecurity and data privacy. Regulators had to adapt quickly to these emerging threats."

Michael listened intently as Jonathan detailed how regulations evolved to address these challenges. "The General Data Protection Regulation (GDPR) in the European Union was a landmark in data privacy. It set strict guidelines on how banks handle personal data, giving consumers more control and ensuring greater transparency."

Jonathan also discussed the importance of anti-money laundering (AML) and know-your-customer (KYC) regulations. "With the rise of digital transactions, it became easier for illicit activities to go undetected. Regulators introduced stricter AML and KYC requirements to combat this, ensuring banks could verify the identities of their customers and monitor transactions for suspicious activity."

Michael was particularly interested in the concept of regulatory technology, or RegTech. "How has technology helped banks comply with these complex regulations?" he asked.

"RegTech has been a game-changer," Jonathan replied. "By leveraging artificial intelligence and machine learning, banks can automate compliance processes, making them more efficient and accurate. This not only reduces the risk of human error but also allows banks to keep up with the ever-changing regulatory landscape."

Jonathan shared an example of a major bank that had implemented a sophisticated RegTech solution. "They used AI to analyze vast amounts of transaction data in real-time, flagging potential compliance issues before they became problems. This proactive approach significantly reduced their regulatory risks."

As their conversation drew to a close, Jonathan emphasized the ongoing nature of regulatory challenges. "The regulatory environment is constantly evolving. As new technologies and business models emerge, so too will the regulations designed to oversee them. It's a continuous process of adaptation and refinement."

Michael left Jonathan's office with a deeper understanding of the regulatory complexities that had shaped modern banking. He realized that navigating this landscape required not only technological innovation but also a keen awareness of the regulatory environment and a commitment to compliance.

Next, Michael planned to explore case studies of legacy banks and challenger banks, hoping to see firsthand how different institutions had responded to these regulatory challenges and adapted to the new financial landscape.

## 1.6: Case Studies: Legacy Banks vs. Challenger Banks

Michael Sawyer's journey through the evolution of banking led him to the bustling streets of London, where he had arranged meetings with executives from both legacy banks and challenger banks. His goal was to gain firsthand insights into how these institutions had navigated the changing landscape of finance.

His first stop was at the headquarters of a prominent legacy bank, nestled in the heart of the financial district. Michael was greeted by Sarah Reynolds, the bank's Chief Strategy Officer, a seasoned executive with a wealth of experience in traditional banking.

"Welcome, Michael," Sarah said, leading him through the sleek, modern lobby adorned with the bank's logo. "We're excited to share our story with you and show you how we're embracing innovation while staying true to our roots."

As they settled into a conference room overlooking the city skyline, Sarah began recounting the bank's long history. "We've been serving customers for over a century, providing trusted financial services through times of prosperity and crisis. Our focus has always been on stability, reliability, and building lasting relationships with our clients."

Michael listened intently as Sarah described the bank's approach to innovation. "We recognize the importance of adapting to changing customer needs and technological advancements. That's why we've invested heavily in digital transformation, upgrading our systems and processes to offer seamless, user-friendly banking experiences."

She shared examples of recent initiatives, such as the launch of a mobile banking app with advanced features like biometric authentication and personalized financial insights. "Our goal is to combine the convenience of digital banking with the personalized service that our customers expect from us."

Michael was impressed by the bank's commitment to innovation while maintaining its core values. As he left the headquarters, he couldn't help but feel a sense of admiration for the legacy institution and its ability to evolve with the times.

His next meeting took him to a trendy co-working space in East London, where he met with the founders of a fast-growing challenger bank. The atmosphere was vibrant and energetic, a stark contrast to the formal ambiance of the legacy bank.

James Cooper, the CEO of the challenger bank, greeted Michael with a firm handshake and a warm smile. "We're thrilled to have you here, Michael," he said, leading him to a communal area filled with young professionals working on laptops.

James began by sharing the bank's origin story, rooted in a desire to disrupt the traditional banking industry. "We saw an opportunity to offer a fresh, innovative alternative to the outdated legacy banks. Our mission is to democratize banking and empower customers with modern, transparent financial services."

He described how the challenger bank had leveraged technology to streamline operations and lower costs, allowing them to offer competitive rates and innovative products. "We're not burdened by legacy systems or bureaucratic red tape. That gives us the agility to quickly adapt to market changes and deliver value to our customers."

Michael was intrigued by the bank's approach to customer experience. James explained how they had built a loyal customer base through personalized service and community engagement. "We're not just a bank; we're a trusted partner on our customers' financial journeys. We listen to their needs and respond with solutions that meet them where they are."

As Michael bid farewell to James and his team, he couldn't help but feel inspired by the challenger bank's bold vision and entrepreneurial spirit. They were rewriting the rules of banking, challenging the status quo, and paving the way for a more inclusive and innovative financial future.

Reflecting on his meetings with both legacy banks and challenger banks, Michael realized that each had its strengths and weaknesses. While legacy banks offered stability and a deep understanding of the industry, challenger banks brought agility and innovation to the table. The key, he realized, was finding a balance between tradition and transformation, embracing the best of both worlds to drive meaningful change in the industry.

Armed with these insights, Michael was eager to continue his exploration of the evolving landscape of finance, knowing that the lessons he had learned from these case studies would guide him on his journey to reinvent banking for the digital age.

# 2

# Chapter 2: Fintech Revolution: Shaping the Future of Finance

## 2.1: Introduction to Fintech

Michael Sawyer's quest to understand the future of finance led him to the vibrant city of New York, where he had arranged a meeting with a group of fintech pioneers. They gathered in a sleek, modern office overlooking the iconic skyline, eager to share their insights into the revolution that was reshaping the financial industry.

As Michael entered the room, he was greeted by a diverse group of entrepreneurs, each with a unique story to tell. The atmosphere crackled with excitement and anticipation as they prepared to delve into the world of fintech.

Natalie Chen, a dynamic young entrepreneur, stepped forward to welcome Michael. "Welcome, Michael. We're thrilled to have you here as we explore the transformative power of fintech."

She began by painting a picture of the fintech landscape,

highlighting its origins and evolution. "Fintech, short for financial technology, is the intersection of finance and technology. It encompasses a wide range of innovations, from mobile payment apps to robo-advisors to blockchain technology."

Michael listened intently as Natalie described how fintech had emerged as a disruptive force, challenging traditional banking models and democratizing access to financial services. "Fintech startups are nimble and innovative, able to quickly adapt to changing market conditions and customer needs. They're reshaping the financial landscape, making it more accessible, efficient, and inclusive."

She shared examples of fintech success stories, from peer-to-peer lending platforms that connected borrowers with investors to mobile banking apps that offered seamless, user-friendly experiences. "These innovations are empowering consumers, giving them greater control over their finances and expanding their options for managing and investing their money."

Michael was captivated by the potential of fintech to drive positive change in the industry. "It's incredible to see how technology is revolutionizing finance and opening up new opportunities for people around the world," he remarked.

Natalie nodded, her eyes sparkling with enthusiasm. "Indeed. But with great innovation comes great responsibility. Fintech also presents challenges, from regulatory compliance to cybersecurity to ethical considerations. As the industry continues to evolve, it's essential that we address these challenges head-on and build a financial ecosystem that is not only innovative but also safe, secure, and ethical."

As their discussion came to a close, Michael felt a renewed sense of purpose. The fintech revolution was not just about creating new products and services; it was about reimagining the entire financial system for the better. He was eager to continue his exploration of fintech, knowing that it held the key to unlocking a more inclusive, efficient, and resilient future for finance.

Armed with the insights and inspiration from his meeting with the fintech pioneers, Michael set out to explore the various facets of the fintech revolution, from payments and lending to wealth management and beyond. He was determined to uncover the innovations that were shaping the future of finance and to learn how he could contribute to this exciting transformation.

## 2.2: Fintech Innovations in Payments

In the heart of San Francisco, Michael Sawyer found himself immersed in the bustling world of fintech startups. He had arranged a series of meetings with entrepreneurs who were leading the charge in revolutionizing payments through innovative fintech solutions.

His first meeting was at a trendy co-working space in the heart of the city, where he was greeted by Sarah Patel, the co-founder of a mobile payment startup. Sarah exuded confidence and enthusiasm as she welcomed Michael into their vibrant office.

"Michael, it's great to have you here," Sarah said, leading him to a communal area filled with young professionals brainstorming ideas. "Let me show you how we're transforming the way people pay for goods and services."

She began by explaining how their mobile payment app had streamlined the payment process, allowing users to make purchases with just a few taps on their smartphones. "Our goal is to make payments faster, easier, and more secure than ever before," Sarah explained. "By leveraging the power of mobile technology, we're empowering consumers to manage their finances on the go."

Michael was intrigued by the simplicity and convenience of the app. "It's incredible to see how technology is changing the way we pay for things," he remarked.

Sarah nodded, her eyes lighting up with excitement. "But that's just the beginning. We're also exploring new payment methods, such as contactless payments and digital wallets, to give consumers even more options for how they pay."

Their conversation turned to the broader impact of fintech innovations in payments. "By reducing reliance on cash and traditional payment methods, fintech is promoting financial inclusion and driving economic growth," Sarah explained. "It's breaking down barriers and giving everyone, regardless of their background or location, access to the financial system."

As Michael left the office, he couldn't help but feel inspired by Sarah's vision and passion for using technology to improve people's lives. He realized that fintech innovations in payments were not just about convenience; they were about empowering individuals and transforming economies.

His next meeting took him to a bustling café, where he met with Max Chen, the founder of a peer-to-peer payment platform. Max shared how their platform had revolutionized the way people send and receive money, allowing users to transfer funds instantly and securely without the need for traditional banks.

"We're democratizing finance and giving people greater control over their money," Max explained. "With our platform, anyone can send money to friends, family, or even strangers with just a few taps on their smartphone. It's revolutionizing the way people think about money."

Michael was impressed by the simplicity and accessibility of the platform. "It's amazing to see how fintech is empowering individuals to take control of their finances," he remarked.

Max nodded, his eyes shining with pride. "But we're not stopping there. We're constantly innovating and exploring new ways to make money more accessible and inclusive for everyone."

As Michael left the café, he reflected on the transformative power of fintech innovations in payments. From mobile payment apps to peer-to-peer platforms, these innovations were not just changing the way people paid for things; they were reshaping the entire financial landscape, opening up new opportunities and possibilities for millions of people around the world.

Armed with these insights, Michael was eager to continue his exploration of the fintech revolution, knowing that the innovations he had witnessed in payments were just the beginning of a much larger transformation in finance.

## 2.3: Peer-to-Peer Lending Platforms

In the heart of London's financial district, Michael Sawyer stepped into a sleek, modern office that buzzed with the energy of innovation. He had arranged a meeting with Emily Wilson, the CEO of a leading peer-to-peer lending platform, eager to learn more about how fintech was reshaping the lending landscape.

Emily greeted Michael with a warm smile, her confidence

and passion evident as she welcomed him into their headquarters.

"Michael, it's a pleasure to have you here," Emily said, leading him to a meeting room with floor-to-ceiling windows that offered panoramic views of the city below. "Let me show you how we're revolutionizing lending through peer-to-peer platforms."

She began by explaining how their platform connected borrowers directly with investors, bypassing traditional banks and intermediaries. "Peer-to-peer lending is about empowering individuals to borrow and lend money on their own terms," Emily explained. "It's a more efficient and transparent way to access credit, with lower fees and better rates for both borrowers and investors."

Michael was fascinated by the simplicity and accessibility of the platform. "It's incredible to see how technology is democratizing access to finance," he remarked.

Emily nodded, her eyes shining with enthusiasm. "But it's not just about convenience. Peer-to-peer lending is also about building communities and fostering trust between borrowers and investors. By connecting people directly, we're creating a more personal and human-centered approach to lending."

Their conversation turned to the broader impact of peer-to-peer lending platforms. "By providing access to credit for underserved communities and small businesses, fintech is driving economic growth and financial inclusion," Emily explained. "It's leveling the playing field and giving everyone, regardless of their background or financial status, the opportunity to achieve their goals."

As Michael left the office, he couldn't help but feel inspired by Emily's vision and determination to use technology for social good. He realized that peer-to-peer lending platforms were not just about disrupting the traditional banking industry; they were about empowering individuals and transforming lives.

His next meeting took him to a bustling café, where he met with Daniel Park, a successful entrepreneur who had used a peer-to-peer lending platform to fund his startup. Daniel shared how the platform had provided him with the capital he needed to launch his business, connecting him with investors who believed in his vision and were willing to support him.

"Peer-to-peer lending changed the game for me," Daniel explained. "It gave me the opportunity to turn my dreams into reality, without having to rely on traditional banks or venture capitalists. It's a more democratic and inclusive way to raise capital, and it's revolutionizing the startup ecosystem."

Michael was impressed by Daniel's story and the transformative impact of peer-to-peer lending on entrepreneurship and innovation. "It's amazing to see how fintech is empowering individuals to take control of their financial futures," he remarked.

As Michael left the café, he reflected on the profound implications of peer-to-peer lending platforms. From providing access to credit for underserved communities to fueling entrepreneurship and innovation, these platforms were not just reshaping the lending landscape; they were reshaping the entire economy, creating new opportunities and possibilities for millions of people around the world.

Armed with these insights, Michael was eager to continue his exploration of the fintech revolution, knowing that the innovations he had witnessed in peer-to-peer lending were just the beginning of a much larger transformation in finance.

## 2.4: Robo-Advisors and Wealth Management

In the heart of Manhattan's financial district, Michael Sawyer entered a sleek, modern office adorned with minimalist decor and state-of-the-art technology. He had arranged a meeting with David Reynolds, the CEO of a leading robo-advisory firm, to delve into the world of fintech-driven wealth management.

David welcomed Michael with a firm handshake, his demeanor exuding confidence and expertise. As they settled into a conference room with panoramic views of the city skyline, David wasted no time in diving into the topic at hand.

"Michael, it's great to have you here," David said, gesturing to the screens displaying real-time market data. "Let me show you how robo-advisors are revolutionizing wealth management."

He began by explaining how their platform used algorithms and machine learning to provide personalized investment advice and portfolio management to clients. "Robo-advisors offer a more efficient and cost-effective alternative to traditional wealth management services," David explained. "By automating investment decisions and rebalancing portfolios, we're able to offer tailored solutions that meet our clients' financial goals while minimizing risk and maximizing returns."

Michael was fascinated by the sophistication and scalability of the platform. "It's incredible to see how technology is democratizing access to wealth management," he remarked.

David nodded, his eyes gleaming with excitement. "But it's not just about accessibility. Robo-advisors also offer transparency and simplicity, making it easier for clients to understand their investments and make informed decisions about their financial future."

Their conversation turned to the broader impact of robo-advisors on the wealth management industry. "By lowering the barriers to entry and reducing fees, fintech is making wealth management more inclusive and accessible to a broader range of investors," David explained. "It's leveling the playing field and empowering individuals to take control of their financial futures."

As Michael left the office, he couldn't help but feel inspired by David's vision and passion for using technology to democratize wealth management. He realized that robo-advisors were not just about disrupting the traditional wealth management industry; they were about empowering individuals and transforming the way people think about investing.

His next meeting took him to a luxurious private club, where he met with Sophia Liu, a successful entrepreneur who had used a robo-advisory platform to grow her wealth. Sophia shared how the platform had provided her with personalized investment advice and helped her build a diversified portfolio that aligned with her financial goals.

"Robo-advisors changed the game for me," Sophia explained. "They gave me the tools and resources I needed to take control of my finances and invest with confidence. It's a more transparent and efficient way to manage wealth, and it's revolutionizing the way people think about investing."

Michael was impressed by Sophia's story and the transformative impact of robo-advisors on individual investors. "It's amazing to see how fintech is empowering individuals to take control of their financial futures," he remarked.

As Michael left the club, he reflected on the profound implications of robo-advisors for wealth management. From providing personalized investment advice to minimizing risk and maximizing returns, these platforms were not just reshaping the wealth management landscape; they were reshaping the entire financial industry, creating new opportunities and possibilities for investors around the world.

Armed with these insights, Michael was eager to continue his exploration of the fintech revolution, knowing that the innovations he had witnessed in robo-advisory were just the beginning of a much larger transformation in finance.

## 2.5: Blockchain and Cryptocurrencies

In the heart of Silicon Valley, Michael Sawyer entered a cutting-edge research facility that hummed with the energy of innovation. He had arranged a meeting with Dr. Emily Johnson, a renowned expert in blockchain technology and cryptocurrencies, to explore the transformative potential of fintech in the realm of digital assets.

Dr. Johnson welcomed Michael with a warm smile, her enthusiasm for the topic evident as she led him into a high-tech conference room adorned with digital screens displaying complex algorithms and cryptographic symbols.

"Michael, it's a pleasure to have you here," Dr. Johnson said, gesturing to the displays. "Let me show you how blockchain and cryptocurrencies are revolutionizing the financial landscape."

She began by explaining the fundamentals of blockchain technology, describing it as a decentralized, immutable ledger that records transactions across a network of computers. "Blockchain has the potential to revolutionize the way we transact and store value," Dr. Johnson explained. "By removing the need for intermediaries and central authorities, it offers greater security, transparency, and efficiency in financial transactions."

Michael was captivated by the potential of blockchain to disrupt traditional financial systems. "It's incredible to see how technology is transforming the way we think about trust and decentralization," he remarked.

Dr. Johnson nodded, her eyes sparkling with excitement. "But the true innovation lies in cryptocurrencies, digital assets that are built on blockchain technology," she continued. "Cryptocurrencies offer a decentralized alternative to traditional fiat currencies, allowing for peer-to-peer transactions without the need for intermediaries."

Their conversation turned to the broader impact of blockchain and cryptocurrencies on the financial industry. "By enabling secure and transparent transactions, fintech is democratizing access to financial services and empowering individuals to take control of their money," Dr. Johnson explained. "It's leveling the playing field and creating new opportunities for financial inclusion and innovation."

As Michael left the research facility, he couldn't help but feel inspired by Dr. Johnson's vision and expertise. He realized that blockchain and cryptocurrencies were not just about disrupting the traditional financial industry; they were about empowering individuals and revolutionizing the way we think about money.

His next meeting took him to a bustling crypto conference, where he met with Jake Thompson, a successful investor who had built his fortune through cryptocurrencies. Jake shared how he had embraced blockchain technology and cryptocurrencies early on, recognizing their potential to reshape the financial landscape.

"Cryptocurrencies changed the game for me," Jake explained.

"They gave me the opportunity to invest in revolutionary technology and participate in a global financial system that's borderless, secure, and transparent. It's a more democratic and inclusive way to manage wealth, and it's revolutionizing the way people think about money."

Michael was impressed by Jake's story and the transformative impact of cryptocurrencies on individual investors. "It's amazing to see how fintech is empowering individuals to take control of their financial futures," he remarked.

As Michael left the conference, he reflected on the profound implications of blockchain and cryptocurrencies for the financial industry. From enabling peer-to-peer transactions to promoting financial inclusion and innovation, these technologies were not just reshaping the financial landscape; they were reshaping the entire economy, creating new opportunities and possibilities for millions of people around the world.

Armed with these insights, Michael was eager to continue his exploration of the fintech revolution, knowing that the innovations he had witnessed in blockchain and cryptocurrencies were just the beginning of a much larger transformation in finance.

## 2.6: The Impact of Fintech on Traditional Banking Models

In the heart of Frankfurt, Michael Sawyer entered a historic bank building that stood as a symbol of traditional finance. He had arranged a meeting with Markus Müller, the CEO of a leading traditional bank, to explore the effects of fintech on established banking models.

Markus greeted Michael with a firm handshake, his demeanor reflecting a mix of curiosity and concern as they settled into his spacious office adorned with classical décor.

"Michael, it's a pleasure to have you here," Markus said, gesturing to the grand surroundings. "Let's discuss how fintech is reshaping the landscape of traditional banking."

He began by acknowledging the disruptive force that fintech had become in the financial industry. "Fintech startups have introduced innovative solutions that challenge the status quo of traditional banking," Markus explained. "From mobile payment apps to robo-advisors to blockchain technology, these innovations are transforming the way customers interact with financial services."

Michael listened intently, recognizing the seismic shift occurring within the industry. "It's clear that fintech is revolutionizing the customer experience and forcing traditional banks to adapt," he remarked.

Markus nodded, his expression thoughtful. "Indeed. Fintech has raised the bar for customer expectations, pushing traditional banks to enhance their digital offerings and improve the efficiency of their operations," he continued. "But it's also created new opportunities for collaboration and partnership between fintech startups and established institutions."

Their conversation turned to the broader implications of fintech on traditional banking models. "By fostering competition and innovation, fintech is driving banks to evolve and innovate in order to stay relevant in a rapidly changing landscape," Markus explained. "It's a transformative process that requires traditional banks to embrace technology and adapt to new ways of doing business."

As Michael left the bank, he couldn't help but feel a sense of urgency and excitement about the future of finance. He realized that fintech was not just a disruptor; it was a catalyst for change that would reshape the entire financial industry.

His next meeting took him to a bustling fintech hub, where he met with Julia Schmidt, the co-founder of a successful fintech startup. Julia shared how her company had partnered with traditional banks to offer innovative solutions that combined the best of both worlds.

"Collaboration is key," Julia explained. "By working together, fintech startups and traditional banks can leverage their respective strengths and expertise to create better products and services for customers."

Michael was impressed by Julia's vision and the potential for collaboration between fintech startups and traditional banks. "It's amazing to see how fintech is driving innovation and reshaping the financial landscape," he remarked.

As Michael left the fintech hub, he reflected on the profound impact of fintech on traditional banking models. From fostering competition and innovation to driving collaboration and partnership, fintech was not just disrupting the industry; it was redefining the very nature of finance itself.

Armed with these insights, Michael was eager to continue his exploration of the fintech revolution, knowing that the innovations he had witnessed were just the beginning of a much larger transformation in finance.

# 3

# Chapter 3: Digital Transformation in Banking

## 3.1: The Shift to Digital Channels

In the heart of New York City, Michael Sawyer stepped into a bustling branch of one of the country's oldest banks. He had arranged a meeting with Jennifer Evans, the head of digital transformation, to explore how banks were adapting to the digital age.

Jennifer welcomed Michael with a warm smile, her enthusiasm for the topic evident as they settled into a sleek meeting room adorned with digital screens and modern furnishings.

"Michael, it's great to have you here," Jennifer said, motioning to the screens displaying the bank's mobile app and online banking portal. "Let me show you how we're embracing digital channels to better serve our customers."

She began by explaining how the bank had invested heavily in digital infrastructure, shifting its focus from traditional brick-and-mortar branches to online and mobile platforms.

## CHAPTER 3: DIGITAL TRANSFORMATION IN BANKING

"The shift to digital channels is not just about convenience; it's about meeting the evolving needs of our customers in an increasingly connected world," Jennifer explained.

Michael nodded, recognizing the importance of digital channels in modern banking. "It's clear that technology is reshaping the way customers interact with financial institutions," he remarked.

Jennifer smiled, her eyes gleaming with excitement. "But it's not just about moving transactions online. It's about creating seamless, personalized experiences that meet our customers' needs at every touchpoint," she continued. "From account management to loan applications to customer support, we're leveraging digital technology to provide a more convenient, efficient, and engaging banking experience."

Their conversation turned to the broader impact of digital transformation on the banking industry. "By embracing digital channels, banks can improve operational efficiency, reduce costs, and drive revenue growth," Jennifer explained. "But more importantly, they can deepen customer relationships and build trust by delivering value-added services that enhance the overall banking experience."

As Michael left the bank, he couldn't help but feel inspired by Jennifer's vision and passion for digital transformation. He realized that the shift to digital channels was not just about keeping up with technological trends; it was about fundamentally reimagining the way banks interacted with their customers and delivered value.

His next meeting took him to a bustling tech startup, where he met with Alex Ramirez, the founder of a digital banking platform. Alex shared how his company was disrupting the traditional banking model by offering a fully digital, mobile-first banking experience that catered to the needs of today's digital-savvy consumers.

"Digital channels are the future of banking," Alex explained. "By leveraging technology, we can offer customers greater convenience, flexibility, and control over their finances, all from the palm of their hand."

Michael was impressed by Alex's vision and the potential of digital banking to transform the industry. "It's amazing to see how technology is reshaping the way we think about banking," he remarked.

As Michael left the startup, he reflected on the profound impact of digital transformation on the banking industry. From shifting transactions online to creating personalized experiences, digital channels were not just changing the way banks operated; they were redefining the very nature of banking itself.

Armed with these insights, Michael was eager to continue his exploration of digital transformation in banking, knowing that the innovations he had witnessed were just the beginning of a much larger revolution in finance.

## 3.2: The Banking Apps: Convenience vs. Security

In the heart of London's financial district, Michael Sawyer entered the headquarters of a prominent bank known for its innovative mobile banking app. He had arranged a meeting with Sarah Lawson, the Chief Information Security Officer, to delve into the delicate balance between convenience and security in digital banking.

Sarah greeted Michael with a firm handshake, her demeanor exuding confidence and expertise as they settled into a high-tech meeting room adorned with cybersecurity posters and monitors displaying real-time threat alerts.

"Michael, it's a pleasure to have you here," Sarah said, motioning to the screens displaying the bank's mobile app interface. "Let's discuss how we're navigating the complex landscape of convenience and security in our digital banking offerings."

She began by highlighting the importance of providing customers with a seamless and intuitive banking experience while ensuring the highest standards of security and protection for their sensitive financial data. "The challenge lies in finding the right balance between convenience and security," Sarah explained. "We want to make banking easy and accessible for our customers, but not at the expense of their safety and privacy."

Michael nodded, recognizing the delicate tightrope that banks had to walk in the digital age. "It's a complex issue with no easy answers," he remarked.

Sarah smiled, her eyes reflecting a mix of determination and caution. "Indeed. Our goal is to leverage cutting-edge technology to enhance convenience without compromising security," she continued. "From biometric authentication to multi-factor authentication to encryption protocols, we're implementing layers of security measures to safeguard our customers' information and prevent unauthorized access."

Their conversation turned to the challenges of balancing convenience and security in the design and development of banking apps. "We're constantly evolving and adapting our security measures to stay ahead of emerging threats and protect against cyberattacks," Sarah explained. "But it's a continuous process that requires vigilance and collaboration across all levels of the organization."

As Michael left the bank, he couldn't help but feel impressed by Sarah's commitment to ensuring the safety and security of customers' financial data. He realized that while convenience was important, it should never come at the expense of security.

His next meeting took him to a cybersecurity conference, where he met with John Park, a renowned cybersecurity expert. John shared his insights on the evolving threat landscape and the importance of implementing robust security measures in digital banking apps to protect against increasingly sophisticated cyber threats.

"Security is paramount," John emphasized. "In today's interconnected world, banks must remain vigilant and proactive in defending against cyberattacks to maintain customer trust and confidence."

Michael was struck by John's words and the critical role that security played in the digital banking landscape. "It's clear that convenience must always be balanced with security," he remarked.

As Michael left the conference, he reflected on the delicate equilibrium between convenience and security in digital banking. From biometric authentication to encryption protocols, banks were continuously innovating and adapting to ensure the safety and security of their customers' financial information.

Armed with these insights, Michael was eager to continue his exploration of digital transformation in banking, knowing that the convergence of convenience and security would shape the future of finance in profound ways.

## 3.3: Artificial Intelligence in Banking Operations

In the heart of Singapore's financial hub, Michael Sawyer entered the headquarters of a leading multinational bank known for its groundbreaking use of artificial intelligence (AI) in banking operations. He had arranged a meeting with Dr. Sophia Chen, the bank's Chief Data Scientist, to explore the transformative power of AI in banking.

Dr. Chen greeted Michael with a warm smile, her passion for AI evident as they settled into a sleek conference room equipped with cutting-edge technology and data visualization tools.

"Michael, it's a pleasure to have you here," Dr. Chen said, gesturing to the screens displaying graphs and charts illustrating the bank's AI-driven analytics. "Let me show you how we're leveraging artificial intelligence to revolutionize banking operations."

She began by explaining how the bank had integrated AI into various aspects of its operations, from customer service to risk management to fraud detection. "Artificial intelligence is transforming the way we do banking," Dr. Chen explained. "By analyzing vast amounts of data in real-time, AI enables us to make faster, more informed decisions and deliver personalized experiences to our customers."

Michael nodded, recognizing the immense potential of AI to drive efficiency and innovation in banking. "It's incredible to see how technology is reshaping the industry," he remarked.

Dr. Chen smiled, her eyes sparkling with excitement. "But AI is not just about automation; it's about augmentation," she continued. "By augmenting human intelligence with machine learning algorithms, we can unlock new insights and opportunities that were previously unimaginable."

Their conversation turned to the broader impact of AI on banking operations. "From chatbots and virtual assistants to predictive analytics and recommendation engines, AI is revolutionizing every aspect of banking," Dr. Chen explained. "It's enabling us to better understand customer behavior, mitigate risk, and drive business growth in ways we never thought possible."

As Michael left the bank, he couldn't help but feel inspired by Dr. Chen's vision and the potential of AI to transform the financial industry. He realized that AI was not just a tool; it was a catalyst for change that would reshape the way banks operated and interacted with their customers.

His next meeting took him to a fintech startup, where he met with James Lee, the founder of an AI-powered personal finance app. James shared how his company was using machine learning algorithms to analyze users' spending habits and provide personalized financial advice and recommendations.

"AI is the future of finance," James explained. "By harnessing the power of data and machine learning, we can empower individuals to make smarter financial decisions and achieve their goals."

Michael was impressed by James's innovative approach and the potential of AI to democratize access to financial services. "It's amazing to see how technology is revolutionizing the way we think about banking," he remarked.

As Michael left the startup, he reflected on the profound impact of AI on banking operations. From enhancing customer experiences to driving operational efficiency, AI was not just reshaping the industry; it was redefining the very nature of banking itself.

Armed with these insights, Michael was eager to continue his exploration of digital transformation in banking, knowing that the innovations he had witnessed were just the beginning of a much larger revolution driven by artificial intelligence.

## 3.4: Big Data and Analytics in Banking

In the heart of Zurich's financial district, Michael Sawyer entered the headquarters of a renowned Swiss bank known for its cutting-edge use of big data and analytics. He had arranged a meeting with Dr. Andreas Müller, the bank's Chief Data Officer, to explore the transformative role of big data in banking operations.

Dr. Müller greeted Michael with a firm handshake, his enthusiasm for data analytics evident as they settled into a state-of-the-art conference room equipped with data visualization dashboards and advanced analytics software.

"Michael, it's a pleasure to have you here," Dr. Müller said, gesturing to the screens displaying real-time data feeds and predictive models. "Let me show you how we're harnessing the power of big data and analytics to drive innovation in banking."

He began by explaining how the bank had amassed vast amounts of data from various sources, including customer transactions, market trends, and social media interactions. "Big data is the lifeblood of modern banking," Dr. Müller explained. "By analyzing this data with advanced analytics techniques, we can uncover valuable insights that inform decision-making and drive business growth."

Michael nodded, recognizing the immense potential of big data to revolutionize banking operations. "It's incredible to see how technology is transforming the industry," he remarked.

Dr. Müller smiled, his eyes shining with excitement. "But big data is not just about quantity; it's about quality," he continued. "By leveraging advanced analytics, including machine learning and artificial intelligence, we can extract meaningful patterns and trends from the data to better understand customer behavior, predict market movements, and optimize business processes."

Their conversation turned to the broader impact of big data and analytics on banking. "From risk management to marketing to customer service, big data is reshaping every aspect of banking," Dr. Müller explained. "It's enabling us to personalize products and services, mitigate risks, and drive operational efficiency in ways we never thought possible."

As Michael left the bank, he couldn't help but feel inspired by Dr. Müller's vision and the potential of big data to transform the financial industry. He realized that big data was not just a tool; it was a strategic asset that would shape the future of banking for years to come.

His next meeting took him to a fintech startup, where he met with Sarah Johnson, the co-founder of a data analytics platform. Sarah shared how her company was helping banks harness the power of big data to gain actionable insights and drive innovation in their operations.

"Big data is the new currency of banking," Sarah explained. "By unlocking the value hidden in the data, banks can gain a competitive edge and deliver superior experiences to their customers."

Michael was impressed by Sarah's innovative approach and the potential of big data to revolutionize the industry. "It's amazing to see how technology is reshaping the way we think about banking," he remarked.

As Michael left the startup, he reflected on the profound impact of big data and analytics on banking operations. From uncovering hidden patterns to driving strategic decision-making, big data was not just reshaping the industry; it was redefining the very nature of banking itself.

Armed with these insights, Michael was eager to continue his exploration of digital transformation in banking, knowing that the innovations he had witnessed were just the beginning of a much larger revolution driven by big data and analytics.

## 3.5: Personalization and Customer Experience

In the heart of Tokyo's financial district, Michael Sawyer stepped into a modern bank branch known for its personalized customer experiences. He had arranged a meeting with Aiko Tanaka, the bank's Chief Customer Experience Officer, to explore the transformative power of personalization in banking.

Aiko greeted Michael with a warm smile, her passion for customer-centricity evident as they settled into a cozy meeting area adorned with sleek furniture and interactive touchscreens.

"Michacl, it's wonderful to have you here," Aiko said, gesturing to the screens displaying customer profiles and personalized product recommendations. "Let me show you how we're leveraging the power of personalization to create tailored experiences for our customers."

She began by explaining how the bank had implemented advanced analytics and machine learning algorithms to analyze customer data and identify individual preferences and behaviors. "Personalization is at the heart of everything we do,"

Aiko explained. "By understanding our customers on a deeper level, we can anticipate their needs and deliver customized solutions that meet their unique requirements."

Michael nodded, recognizing the importance of personalized experiences in today's competitive banking landscape. "It's impressive to see how technology is reshaping the way banks interact with their customers," he remarked.

Aiko smiled, her eyes sparkling with enthusiasm. "But personalization is not just about recommending products; it's about building meaningful relationships," she continued. "By providing personalized advice and support, we can foster trust and loyalty among our customers, driving long-term satisfaction and retention."

Their conversation turned to the broader impact of personalization on customer experience in banking. "From tailored product offerings to proactive financial guidance to personalized marketing campaigns, personalization is revolutionizing every touchpoint of the customer journey," Aiko explained. "It's enabling us to create seamless, intuitive experiences that delight and engage our customers at every step."

As Michael left the bank, he couldn't help but feel inspired by Aiko's vision and the potential of personalization to transform the financial industry. He realized that personalization was not just a trend; it was a strategic imperative that would shape the future of banking for years to come.

His next meeting took him to a fintech startup, where he met with David Kim, the CEO of a personal finance app. David shared how his company was using artificial intelligence and predictive analytics to deliver personalized financial advice and recommendations to users.

"Personalization is the future of finance," David explained.

"By understanding users' financial goals and preferences, we can provide tailored insights and recommendations that empower them to make smarter decisions and achieve their objectives."

Michael was impressed by David's innovative approach and the potential of personalization to revolutionize the industry. "It's incredible to see how technology is reshaping the way we think about banking," he remarked.

As Michael left the startup, he reflected on the profound impact of personalization on customer experience in banking. From anticipating needs to delivering tailored solutions, personalization was not just reshaping the industry; it was redefining the very nature of banking itself.

Armed with these insights, Michael was eager to continue his exploration of digital transformation in banking, knowing that the innovations he had witnessed were just the beginning of a much larger revolution driven by personalization and customer experience.

## 3.6: Cybersecurity Challenges in the Digital Era

In the heart of Washington, D.C., Michael Sawyer entered the headquarters of a leading cybersecurity firm specializing in financial services. He had arranged a meeting with Rebecca Johnson, the company's Chief Security Officer, to explore the critical role of cybersecurity in the digital transformation of banking.

Rebecca greeted Michael with a firm handshake, her demeanor exuding confidence and expertise as they settled into a high-tech meeting room equipped with monitors displaying real-time threat intelligence feeds.

"Michael, it's great to have you here," Rebecca said, motioning to the screens. "Let me show you how we're tackling the cybersecurity challenges facing the banking industry in the digital era."

She began by explaining how the rapid digitization of banking operations had led to an unprecedented increase in cyber threats and vulnerabilities. "Cybersecurity is the cornerstone of trust in the digital age," Rebecca explained. "As banks embrace new technologies and channels, they become prime targets for cyberattacks seeking to exploit weaknesses and compromise sensitive information."

Michael nodded, recognizing the critical importance of cybersecurity in safeguarding customers' financial assets and data. "It's clear that banks must remain vigilant in the face of evolving threats," he remarked.

Rebecca smiled, her eyes reflecting a mix of determination and caution. "Indeed. Our goal is to stay one step ahead of cybercriminals by implementing robust security measures and adopting a proactive approach to threat detection and response," she continued. "From encryption and multi-factor authentication to intrusion detection and incident response, we're working tirelessly to protect our clients' digital assets and preserve trust in the financial system."

Their conversation turned to the broader impact of cybersecurity on the digital transformation of banking. "Cybersecurity is not just a technical challenge; it's a strategic imperative," Rebecca explained. "By prioritizing cybersecurity and building a culture of security awareness, banks can mitigate risks, enhance resilience, and maintain customer confidence in an increasingly interconnected world."

As Michael left the cybersecurity firm, he couldn't help

but feel impressed by Rebecca's dedication to protecting the integrity of the financial system. He realized that cybersecurity was not just a technology issue; it was a fundamental pillar of trust that underpinned the digital transformation of banking.

His next meeting took him to a regulatory agency, where he met with Thomas Anderson, the head of cybersecurity regulation. Thomas shared his insights on the regulatory landscape and the importance of collaboration between banks, regulators, and cybersecurity firms to address emerging threats and ensure the resilience of the financial sector.

"Cybersecurity is a shared responsibility," Thomas emphasized. "By working together, we can strengthen the cybersecurity posture of banks and protect the stability and integrity of the financial system."

Michael was struck by Thomas's words and the collaborative efforts underway to address cybersecurity challenges in the digital era. "It's reassuring to see stakeholders coming together to tackle this critical issue," he remarked.

As Michael left the regulatory agency, he reflected on the profound impact of cybersecurity on the digital transformation of banking. From protecting sensitive data to preserving trust in the financial system, cybersecurity was not just a technical challenge; it was a strategic imperative that required constant vigilance and collaboration.

Armed with these insights, Michael was eager to continue his exploration of digital transformation in banking, knowing that cybersecurity would play a central role in shaping the future of finance in the digital era.

# 4

# Chapter 4: Open Banking and API Economy

## 4.1: Understanding Open Banking

In the bustling streets of New York City, Michael Sawyer stepped into a modern coworking space where fintech innovators congregated to revolutionize the financial industry. He had arranged a meeting with Rachel Evans, a prominent fintech entrepreneur, to delve into the concept of open banking and its implications for the future of finance.

Rachel greeted Michael with a warm smile, her enthusiasm for open banking evident as they settled into a vibrant meeting area adorned with whiteboards covered in diagrams and schematics.

"Michael, it's a pleasure to have you here," Rachel said, gesturing to the whiteboards. "Let me walk you through the transformative power of open banking and how it's reshaping the financial landscape."

She began by explaining the concept of open banking

and its core principles of data sharing, transparency, and collaboration. "Open banking represents a seismic shift in the way financial services are delivered and consumed," Rachel explained. "By opening up access to customer data and banking infrastructure through standardized APIs, open banking empowers consumers to securely share their financial information with third-party providers, enabling them to access a wider range of products and services tailored to their needs."

Michael nodded, recognizing the potential of open banking to foster innovation and competition in the financial industry. "It's fascinating to see how technology is democratizing access to financial services," he remarked.

Rachel smiled, her eyes sparkling with excitement. "But open banking is not just about access; it's about empowerment," she continued. "By giving consumers greater control over their financial data, open banking enables them to make more informed decisions, manage their finances more effectively, and ultimately achieve their financial goals."

Their conversation turned to the broader implications of open banking for banks, fintech startups, and consumers alike. "From new revenue streams and business models to enhanced customer experiences and financial inclusion, open banking is revolutionizing every aspect of the financial ecosystem," Rachel explained. "It's driving innovation, fostering collaboration, and unlocking opportunities that were previously unimaginable."

As Michael left the coworking space, he couldn't help but feel inspired by Rachel's vision and the transformative potential of open banking to reshape the financial industry. He realized that open banking was not just a trend; it was a paradigm shift that would redefine the very nature of finance in the digital age.

His next meeting took him to a regulatory agency, where he met with Emily Thompson, the head of open banking regulation. Emily shared her insights on the regulatory landscape and the importance of fostering a supportive environment for open banking innovation while ensuring consumer protection and data privacy.

"Open banking holds tremendous promise, but it also presents unique challenges and risks," Emily emphasized. "By establishing clear regulatory frameworks and standards, we can promote innovation while safeguarding consumers' rights and interests."

Michael was struck by Emily's words and the collaborative efforts underway to promote open banking innovation while ensuring regulatory compliance and consumer protection. "It's reassuring to see regulators and industry stakeholders working together to unlock the full potential of open banking," he remarked.

As Michael left the regulatory agency, he reflected on the profound impact of open banking on the future of finance. From fostering innovation to empowering consumers, open banking was not just a concept; it was a catalyst for change that would redefine the financial landscape for generations to come.

Armed with these insights, Michael was eager to continue his exploration of open banking and the API economy, knowing that the innovations he had witnessed were just the beginning of a much larger revolution driven by data sharing, collaboration, and empowerment.

## 4.2: The Role of APIs in Banking

In the heart of London's financial district, Michael Sawyer entered the headquarters of a leading bank known for its pioneering use of APIs in banking services. He had arranged a meeting with Mark Roberts, the bank's Chief Technology Officer, to explore the transformative role of APIs in reshaping the financial landscape.

Mark greeted Michael with a firm handshake, his passion for technology evident as they settled into a sleek meeting room equipped with screens displaying real-time API usage metrics and developer engagement statistics.

"Michael, it's great to have you here," Mark said, gesturing to the screens. "Let me show you how we're leveraging APIs to drive innovation and create new opportunities in banking."

He began by explaining the concept of APIs and their significance in enabling seamless communication and integration between different software applications and systems. "APIs are the building blocks of open banking," Mark explained. "By providing standardized interfaces for accessing banking data and functionality, APIs empower developers to build innovative products and services that enhance the customer experience and drive business growth."

Michael nodded, recognizing the transformative potential of APIs to foster collaboration and innovation in the financial industry. "It's incredible to see how technology is breaking down barriers and opening up new possibilities in banking," he remarked.

Mark smiled, his eyes lighting up with excitement. "But APIs are not just about technical integration; they're about fostering ecosystems," he continued. "By opening up our APIs to third-party developers, we can create vibrant ecosystems of fintech startups, partners, and innovators who can leverage our banking infrastructure to build innovative solutions that address evolving customer needs and preferences."

Their conversation turned to the broader implications of APIs for banks, fintech startups, and consumers alike. "From enabling seamless payments and account aggregation to facilitating personalized financial advice and product recommendations, APIs are revolutionizing every aspect of the banking experience," Mark explained. "They're driving innovation, fostering collaboration, and unlocking value that benefits everyone in the ecosystem."

As Michael left the bank, he couldn't help but feel inspired by Mark's vision and the transformative potential of APIs to reshape the financial industry. He realized that APIs were not just a technology; they were a catalyst for innovation and collaboration that would redefine the very nature of banking in the digital age.

His next meeting took him to a fintech startup, where he met with Sarah Johnson, the CEO of a financial data aggregation platform. Sarah shared how her company was leveraging APIs to aggregate data from multiple banks and financial institutions, providing users with a comprehensive view of their finances and empowering them to make better financial decisions.

"APIs are the lifeblood of our platform," Sarah explained. "By leveraging APIs to access banking data securely and efficiently, we can provide users with valuable insights and tools that help them take control of their finances and achieve their goals."

Michael was impressed by Sarah's innovative approach and the potential of APIs to democratize access to financial services.

"It's amazing to see how technology is reshaping the way we think about banking," he remarked.

As Michael left the startup, he reflected on the profound impact of APIs on the future of finance. From fostering collaboration to driving innovation, APIs were not just a technical tool; they were a fundamental enabler of the open banking revolution that was reshaping the financial landscape for generations to come.

Armed with these insights, Michael was eager to continue his exploration of open banking and the API economy, knowing that the innovations he had witnessed were just the beginning of a much larger revolution driven by collaboration, interoperability, and innovation.

## 4.3: Benefits for Consumers and Businesses

Michael stood before a packed auditorium at a fintech conference in San Francisco. The audience, a mix of bankers, tech entrepreneurs, and regulators, buzzed with anticipation. Michael's reputation as a visionary in the banking sector had drawn them here, eager to hear his insights on the latest developments in open banking.

"Good afternoon, everyone," Michael began, his voice clear and confident. "Today, we're going to dive into one of the most transformative aspects of modern finance: the benefits of open banking for consumers and businesses."

As the lights dimmed, the screen behind him lit up with a dynamic infographic illustrating the interconnectedness of traditional banks, fintech companies, and third-party providers through open APIs.

"Open banking is more than just a technical innovation,"

Michael continued. "It's a paradigm shift that puts the power back in the hands of consumers and drives efficiency and growth for businesses."

## *Empowering Consumers*

In a bustling café in downtown New York, Clara, a young professional, sipped her coffee while scrolling through her banking app. Unlike the clunky interfaces of old, her app was sleek and intuitive, integrating multiple financial services in one place.

Clara tapped on the 'Personal Finance' section, where she could view all her accounts, from different banks, in a single dashboard. This holistic view allowed her to track her spending, set savings goals, and receive personalized financial advice.

"Hey, Clara," her friend Mark called out, sliding into the seat opposite her. "You seem deep in thought."

"Just marveling at how much easier managing my finances has become," Clara replied. "Thanks to open banking, I can control everything from one app. It even suggested a better savings account based on my spending habits."

Mark leaned in, intrigued. "Really? I've been struggling to keep track of my investments and expenses. Maybe I should give it a try."

Clara smiled, knowing that this convenience and empowerment were just the beginning of what open banking could offer consumers like her.

## Boosting Businesses

Across the Atlantic, in a small London office, Emma, the owner of a growing e-commerce startup, was in a meeting with her CFO, Raj. They were discussing the company's financial strategies when Emma's phone buzzed with a notification.

"It's from our banking app," she explained, swiping to open the message. "We've been pre-approved for a business loan, with terms tailored to our cash flow and growth projections."

Raj nodded approvingly. "That's the power of open banking. By allowing our bank to access our financial data, we've streamlined the loan approval process and secured better terms. It's a game-changer for our working capital management."

Emma leaned back, her mind racing with possibilities. "With this loan, we can invest in new inventory and marketing, and expand our reach. This wouldn't have been possible so quickly with traditional banking."

## The Wider Impact

Back at the conference, Michael elaborated on these examples. "For consumers, open banking means more control, better financial products, and enhanced transparency. For businesses, it translates to improved cash flow management, easier access to credit, and the ability to offer innovative services."

He paused, letting the weight of his words sink in. "But the benefits extend even further. By fostering competition and innovation, open banking can lead to lower costs and better services across the board."

Michael clicked to the next slide, showcasing case studies from around the world. "In Brazil, open banking has driven financial inclusion, bringing banking services to millions of unbanked citizens. In Europe, it's fueling competition and innovation, pushing traditional banks to evolve."

The audience was captivated, seeing the potential of open banking through Michael's eyes. He concluded, "Open banking is not just a trend; it's the future. And it's up to us to harness its potential for the benefit of all."

The room erupted in applause. Michael stepped back, satisfied. He had painted a vivid picture of a world where open banking bridged gaps, empowered individuals, and propelled businesses into a new era of financial prosperity.

As the crowd dispersed, Michael couldn't help but feel a surge of optimism. The journey of transformation was just beginning, and the possibilities were endless.

## 4.4: Challenges and Risks of Open Banking

Michael returned to the stage after a brief break, his mind filled with the positive feedback from the morning session. However, he knew that the discussion of open banking wouldn't be complete without addressing the darker side of this transformation.

"While the benefits of open banking are substantial," Michael began, "it's crucial to acknowledge and understand the challenges and risks associated with it. Only by confronting these issues head-on can we ensure a secure and sustainable future for this new banking paradigm."

## *The Security Dilemma*

In a high-rise office building in Singapore, James, the Chief Information Security Officer (CISO) of a major bank, was pacing back and forth. His team had just discovered a potential security breach involving one of their third-party API providers.

"We've found a vulnerability in the API used for transaction data," his lead security analyst reported. "If exploited, it could allow unauthorized access to sensitive customer information."

James's heart raced. "We need to shut it down immediately and inform our partners. Start an investigation to determine the extent of the breach."

As the team scrambled into action, James reflected on the security dilemma posed by open banking. Integrating multiple APIs increased the attack surface, making it more challenging to protect against cyber threats. Despite rigorous vetting processes, vulnerabilities could still slip through, posing significant risks to both the bank and its customers.

## *Privacy Concerns*

In Berlin, Anna, a data privacy advocate, was preparing for a televised debate on the implications of open banking. Opposite her sat Marcus, a spokesperson for a leading fintech company.

"Open banking inherently involves sharing sensitive financial data across multiple platforms," Anna argued passionately. "This raises serious privacy concerns. How can consumers be sure their data is safe and won't be misused?"

Marcus responded confidently, "We have strict data protection measures and comply with all regulatory standards. Open banking offers transparency and control to consumers over their data."

Anna wasn't convinced. "Regulations like GDPR are a start, but enforcement is inconsistent, and breaches still occur. Consumers need to be aware of the risks and have robust mechanisms to manage their data consent."

The debate highlighted the tension between innovation and privacy. While open banking promised convenience and improved services, it also demanded heightened vigilance to protect consumer data and ensure privacy rights were respected.

*Regulatory Hurdles*

In Washington, D.C., a committee room buzzed with intense discussions. Policymakers, bankers, and tech leaders had gathered to discuss the regulatory framework for open banking in the United States.

Senator Thompson, a staunch advocate for consumer protection, voiced his concerns. "Open banking is an exciting development, but we need robust regulations to protect consumers and ensure fair competition. Without clear guidelines, we risk creating a Wild West in the financial sector."

Michael, representing the fintech community, responded, "We agree on the need for regulation, Senator. However, it's vital that these regulations foster innovation rather than stifle it. We need a balanced approach that safeguards consumers while allowing the industry to evolve."

The discussions underscored the complex regulatory landscape of open banking. Crafting policies that protected consumers, encouraged innovation, and maintained financial stability was a delicate balancing act, fraught with challenges.

## Technical and Operational Challenges

In Mumbai, Riya, the CTO of an emerging neobank, faced technical difficulties as her team worked to integrate various third-party APIs. "We're experiencing compatibility issues with some of the older banking systems," her lead developer reported.

Riya sighed. "We knew this would be challenging. Open banking requires seamless integration, but legacy systems are not always designed for this level of interoperability. We need to find a way to bridge these technological gaps."

The team huddled, brainstorming solutions to ensure smooth API integration and optimal performance. Technical challenges were inevitable in the transition to open banking, demanding innovative solutions and constant adaptation.

## Consumer Trust and Education

Back at the conference in San Francisco, Michael addressed the audience once more. "Perhaps the most significant challenge is consumer trust and education. For open banking to succeed, consumers must trust that their data is secure and understand how to manage their financial information responsibly."

He shared a story about Emma, the e-commerce startup owner, who initially hesitated to adopt open banking due to concerns about data security. "It took time and education to help her see the benefits and feel confident in the system. Building trust requires transparency, robust security measures, and ongoing consumer education."

Michael concluded, "While the road ahead is fraught with challenges, I firmly believe that with collaboration, innovation, and a commitment to security and privacy, we can overcome these obstacles. Open banking has the potential to revolutionize finance, but we must navigate these challenges wisely."

As the audience applauded, Michael felt a renewed sense of purpose. The journey to fully realizing the potential of open banking was complex, but by addressing these challenges head-on, they could pave the way for a safer, more inclusive financial future.

## 4.5: Global Perspectives on Open Banking

In the heart of Singapore's financial hub, Michael Sawyer entered a bustling conference hall where experts from around the world had gathered to discuss the global impact of open banking. He had arranged to attend a panel discussion featuring leading figures in the field, each offering unique perspectives on the transformative power of open banking on a global scale.

The panel was moderated by Dr. Sophia Chen, a renowned fintech researcher, who welcomed Michael and the audience with a warm smile. "Welcome, everyone, to this insightful discussion on the global perspectives on open banking," Dr. Chen began. "Today, we have with us a distinguished panel of experts who will share their insights and experiences on how open banking is reshaping the financial landscape worldwide."

The panelists included Alejandro Santos, the CEO of a leading bank in Latin America; Zhang Wei, the head of a fintech startup in China; and Anne-Marie Dupont, a regulatory expert from the European Union.

Alejandro spoke passionately about the transformative impact of open banking in Latin America, where regulatory initiatives were driving innovation and competition in the financial sector. "Open banking has the potential to empower consumers and drive economic growth in our region," he explained. "By fostering collaboration between banks and fintechs, we can create new opportunities and deliver innovative solutions that meet the evolving needs of our customers."

Zhang Wei shared his experiences from China, where technological innovation and consumer demand were driving rapid adoption of open banking principles. "In China, open banking is not just a trend; it's a fundamental shift in the way financial services are delivered and consumed," he said. "By leveraging APIs and digital platforms, we can create seamless, integrated ecosystems that provide users with personalized, convenient, and secure financial experiences."

Anne-Marie offered insights from the European Union, where regulatory initiatives such as the Payment Services Directive (PSD2) had paved the way for open banking innovation. "In Europe, open banking is transforming the financial landscape by promoting competition, innovation, and consumer choice," she explained. "By mandating banks to open up their APIs to third-party providers, we're enabling new players to enter the market, driving down costs, and improving the quality of services for consumers."

As the panel discussion drew to a close, Dr. Chen thanked the panelists for their valuable insights and contributions. "Today, we've heard from experts from different regions of the world, each offering a unique perspective on the transformative power of open banking," she remarked. "From Latin America to China to Europe and beyond, open banking is reshaping the financial landscape and driving innovation, collaboration, and consumer empowerment on a global scale."

As Michael left the conference hall, he couldn't help but feel inspired by the diverse perspectives and experiences shared by the panelists. He realized that open banking was not just a concept; it was a global movement that was reshaping the financial industry and unlocking new opportunities for innovation and growth around the world.

Armed with these insights, Michael was eager to continue his exploration of open banking and the API economy, knowing that the global perspectives he had encountered were just the beginning of a much larger revolution driven by collaboration, interoperability, and innovation across borders.

## 4.6: Future Trends and Opportunities

In the heart of San Francisco's innovation district, Michael Sawyer found himself in a bustling conference hall, attending a keynote address by Dr. Emily Chen, a leading futurist specializing in financial technology. The topic of her presentation: future trends and opportunities in open banking.

Dr. Chen stood on stage, her presence commanding attention as she began her address. "Good morning, everyone. Today, I want to take you on a journey into the future of open banking and explore the trends and opportunities that lie ahead."

She started by highlighting the rapid pace of technological innovation and its impact on the financial industry. "In the coming years, we can expect to see a continued convergence of technology and finance, driven by advancements in artificial intelligence, blockchain, and quantum computing," she explained. "These technologies will not only enhance the security and efficiency of open banking but also enable new forms of financial services and business models that we can't even imagine today."

Michael listened intently, captivated by Dr. Chen's vision of the future. He realized that the possibilities were endless, and the future of open banking was filled with opportunities for innovation and growth.

Dr. Chen continued by discussing the rise of decentralized finance (DeFi) and its potential to disrupt traditional banking models. "DeFi has the potential to democratize access to financial services and eliminate intermediaries, allowing individuals to access banking services directly on blockchain-based platforms," she said. "This presents both challenges and opportunities for traditional banks, as they navigate this new decentralized landscape and explore ways to collaborate with DeFi platforms or integrate blockchain technology into their operations."

Michael nodded, recognizing the transformative potential of DeFi to reshape the financial industry and create new opportunities for innovation and inclusion.

As Dr. Chen concluded her address, she left the audience with a thought-provoking question: "As we look to the future of open banking, what role will you play in shaping the next chapter of this transformative journey?"

Michael left the conference hall feeling inspired and energized by Dr. Chen's insights. He realized that the future of open banking was not just about technology; it was about vision, innovation, and collaboration. As he walked through the bustling streets of San Francisco, he couldn't help but feel excited about the opportunities that lay ahead and the role he could play in shaping the future of finance.

Armed with Dr. Chen's insights, Michael was eager to continue his exploration of open banking and the API economy, knowing that the future was full of possibilities and opportunities for those willing to embrace change and lead the way into tomorrow.

# 5

# Chapter 5: The Rise of Neobanks and Challenger Banks

## 5.1: Defining Neobanks and Challenger Banks

In the heart of London's financial district, Michael Sawyer entered a sleek, modern office space adorned with minimalist decor and bustling with activity. He had arranged to meet with Sarah Thompson, the co-founder and CEO of a leading neobank, to delve into the phenomenon of neobanks and challenger banks and understand their role in reshaping the banking landscape.

Sarah greeted Michael with a warm smile, her enthusiasm for innovation evident as they settled into a cozy meeting area overlooking the city skyline.

"Michael, it's great to have you here," Sarah said, pouring them both cups of steaming coffee. "Let's dive into the world of neobanks and challenger banks and explore how they're disrupting the traditional banking industry."

She began by defining neobanks and challenger banks as

innovative financial institutions that leverage technology to offer digital-first banking experiences tailored to the needs of modern consumers. "Neobanks and challenger banks are shaking up the status quo by challenging traditional banking models and offering customers a fresh, user-centric approach to banking," Sarah explained. "They prioritize simplicity, transparency, and affordability, delivering seamless digital experiences that resonate with today's tech-savvy consumers."

Michael nodded, intrigued by Sarah's insights. He realized that neobanks and challenger banks were more than just financial institutions; they were agents of change, ushering in a new era of banking built on innovation and customer empowerment.

Sarah continued by discussing the key differences between neobanks and challenger banks. "While neobanks are typically digital-only banks that operate without physical branches, challenger banks may have a hybrid model, combining digital channels with a limited number of physical locations," she explained. "Both types of banks share a common goal: to challenge the dominance of traditional banks and offer consumers a more agile, customer-centric alternative."

Their conversation turned to the broader impact of neobanks and challenger banks on the banking industry and society as a whole. "From fostering competition and driving innovation to promoting financial inclusion and empowering consumers, neobanks and challenger banks are reshaping the banking landscape in profound ways," Sarah emphasized. "They're challenging outdated practices, driving down costs, and raising the bar for customer experience, forcing traditional banks to adapt or risk being left behind."

As Michael left the neobank's office, he couldn't help but feel inspired by Sarah's passion and vision for the future of banking. He realized that neobanks and challenger banks were not just disruptors; they were pioneers, leading the charge towards a more inclusive, customer-centric banking ecosystem.

Armed with Sarah's insights, Michael was eager to continue his exploration of neobanks and challenger banks, knowing that they held the key to unlocking new opportunities and driving positive change in the financial industry and beyond.

## 5.2: Disrupting the Status Quo: Neobanks vs. Traditional Banks

In the heart of New York City, Michael Sawyer found himself in a boardroom at a traditional bank, surrounded by executives discussing the rise of neobanks and challenger banks. He had arranged to attend a high-level meeting led by James Robertson, the CEO of the bank, to gain insights into how traditional banks were responding to the disruptive forces of the digital age.

James addressed the room with a commanding presence, his voice resonating with authority as he began his presentation. "Good morning, everyone. Today, we're going to discuss the impact of neobanks and challenger banks on the traditional banking industry and explore how we can adapt and thrive in this rapidly evolving landscape."

He started by acknowledging the rise of neobanks and challenger banks as formidable competitors that were challenging the dominance of traditional banks. "Neobanks and challenger banks are disrupting the status quo by offering customers innovative, digital-first banking experiences that are simple, transparent, and affordable," James explained. "They're leveraging technology to streamline operations, reduce costs, and deliver personalized services that resonate with today's consumers."

Michael listened intently, realizing the urgency of the situation as traditional banks grappled with the need to innovate and adapt in the face of increasing competition. He recognized that neobanks and challenger banks were not just disruptors; they were catalysts for change, forcing traditional banks to rethink their business models and customer strategies.

James continued by discussing the key areas where neobanks and challenger banks were outperforming traditional banks, such as digital customer experience, product innovation, and agility. "Neobanks and challenger banks have a competitive edge when it comes to meeting the evolving needs and preferences of modern consumers," he said. "They're able to move quickly, iterate rapidly, and experiment with new ideas, giving them a significant advantage in today's fast-paced digital environment."

As the meeting drew to a close, James emphasized the importance of embracing innovation and adopting a customer-centric mindset to stay competitive in an increasingly digital world. "We need to think like neobanks and challenger banks," he declared. "We need to prioritize innovation, agility, and customer experience if we want to remain relevant and thrive in the years to come."

Michael left the boardroom feeling energized by James's vision and the determination of the traditional bank to adapt and evolve in the face of disruption. He realized that neobanks and challenger banks were not just competitors; they were driving positive change in the industry, pushing traditional banks to innovate and raise the bar for customer experience.

Armed with James's insights, Michael was eager to continue his exploration of neobanks and challenger banks, knowing that they were not just disruptors; they were shaping the future of banking and redefining the relationship between banks and their customers.

## 5.3: Business Models and Revenue Streams

In the heart of San Francisco's financial district, Michael Sawyer found himself in a sleek, modern office space adorned with vibrant artwork and buzzing with creative energy. He had arranged to meet with David Nguyen, the co-founder and CFO of a leading neobank, to delve into the innovative business models and revenue streams driving the success of neobanks and challenger banks.

David welcomed Michael with a warm smile, his enthusiasm for innovation evident as they settled into a cozy meeting area overlooking the city skyline.

"Michael, it's great to have you here," David said, pouring them both cups of artisanal coffee. "Let's dive into the world of neobanks and challenger banks and explore how their business models and revenue streams are disrupting the traditional banking industry."

He began by explaining how neobanks and challenger banks had embraced digital-first business models that prioritized simplicity, transparency, and customer-centricity. "Unlike traditional banks, which rely heavily on physical branches and legacy systems, neobanks and challenger banks leverage technology to deliver seamless, personalized banking experiences that resonate with today's consumers," David explained. "They offer innovative products and services, such as fee-free banking, real-time payments, and AI-driven financial advice, that differentiate them from traditional banks and attract tech-savvy customers."

Michael nodded, impressed by the ingenuity and agility of neobanks and challenger banks in designing business models that catered to the needs and preferences of modern consumers. He realized that their focus on innovation and customer experience was driving their success and challenging traditional banks to adapt or risk being left behind.

David continued by discussing the diverse revenue streams of neobanks and challenger banks, which often included a combination of interchange fees, subscription fees, lending revenue, and partnerships with fintechs and other service providers. "Neobanks and challenger banks have embraced a range of revenue models that allow them to monetize their customer base while offering value-added services that drive engagement and loyalty," he said. "By diversifying their revenue streams and embracing new business opportunities, they're able to build sustainable, profitable businesses that are resilient to market changes and disruptions."

Their conversation turned to the broader impact of neobanks and challenger banks on the banking industry and society as a whole. "From fostering competition and driving innovation to promoting financial inclusion and empowering consumers, neobanks and challenger banks are reshaping the banking landscape in profound ways," David emphasized. "They're challenging outdated practices, driving down costs, and raising the bar for customer experience, forcing traditional banks to adapt or risk being left behind."

As Michael left the neobank's office, he couldn't help but feel inspired by David's vision and the innovative spirit of neobanks and challenger banks. He realized that they were not just disruptors; they were pioneers, leading the charge towards a more inclusive, customer-centric banking ecosystem.

Armed with David's insights, Michael was eager to continue his exploration of neobanks and challenger banks, knowing that they held the key to unlocking new opportunities and driving positive change in the financial industry and beyond.

## 5.4: Neobanks Around the World: Case Studies

In a bustling co-working space in London, Michael Sawyer found himself surrounded by the vibrant energy of innovative startups and entrepreneurs. He had arranged to meet with Emma Jones, the CEO of Bank X, a leading neobank that had gained prominence for its disruptive approach to banking.

Emma greeted Michael with a warm smile, her passion for innovation evident as they settled into a cozy meeting area.

"Michael, it's great to have you here," Emma said, pouring them both cups of freshly brewed tea. "Let's dive into the world of neobanks and explore how Bank X is reshaping the banking landscape."

She began by sharing the story of Bank X, a digital-only neobank that had quickly gained traction in the UK market by offering fee-free banking and innovative features such as instant payments and budgeting tools. "Bank X was founded with a mission to make banking fairer, simpler, and more accessible for everyone," Emma explained. "We've leveraged technology to streamline operations, reduce costs, and deliver a seamless digital banking experience that resonates with today's consumers."

Michael listened intently as Emma detailed Bank X's rapid

growth and expansion plans, which included launching new products and entering new markets across Europe and beyond. He was impressed by the neobank's customer-centric approach and its commitment to driving positive change in the banking industry.

Their conversation then turned to Monzo, another prominent neobank that had disrupted the UK banking landscape with its colorful branding and innovative features. "Monzo has redefined the banking experience for millions of customers with its user-friendly app, real-time notifications, and innovative budgeting tools," Emma remarked. "They've built a loyal following of customers who appreciate their transparent fees, intuitive interface, and commitment to financial education."

As they discussed neobanks from around the world, including Chime in the US, N26 in Germany, and Revolut in Europe, Michael realized the global impact of these innovative financial institutions. "Neobanks are not just disrupting the traditional banking industry; they're setting new standards for customer experience, innovation, and transparency," he remarked.

Emma nodded in agreement, emphasizing the importance of collaboration and knowledge sharing among neobanks to drive continued growth and innovation in the industry. "By learning from each other's successes and challenges, we can collectively push the boundaries of what's possible in banking and create a more inclusive, customer-centric financial ecosystem," she said.

As Michael left the co-working space, he couldn't help but feel inspired by Emma's vision and the global impact of neobanks like Bank X. He realized that they were not just disruptors; they were pioneers, leading the charge towards a more inclusive, transparent, and innovative future of banking.

Armed with insights from Bank X and other neobanks around the world, Michael was eager to continue his exploration of the neobank phenomenon, knowing that they held the key to unlocking new opportunities and driving positive change in the financial industry and beyond.

## 5.5: Partnerships and Collaborations with Neobanks

In the heart of Silicon Valley, Michael Sawyer found himself in a bustling conference room at a leading fintech accelerator, surrounded by executives from traditional banks and innovative startups. He had arranged to attend a roundtable discussion on partnerships and collaborations between traditional banks and neobanks, led by Sarah Patel, the head of partnerships at a prominent neobank.

Sarah welcomed Michael with a warm smile, her passion for collaboration evident as she addressed the group. "Good morning, everyone. Today, we're going to explore how partnerships and collaborations between traditional banks and neobanks can drive innovation, enhance customer experience, and create value for all stakeholders."

She began by sharing the story of a recent partnership between her neobank and a traditional bank, which had resulted in the launch of a co-branded savings account aimed at millennials. "By combining the agility and innovation of our neobank with the scale and expertise of the traditional bank, we were able to create a product that resonated with a new generation of customers," Sarah explained. "It was a win-win for both parties, as it allowed us to leverage each other's strengths and reach new markets more effectively."

Michael listened intently as Sarah detailed the benefits of

partnerships between traditional banks and neobanks, which included access to new customer segments, enhanced product offerings, and shared resources and expertise. He realized that collaboration was key to driving innovation and staying competitive in an increasingly digital and customer-centric banking landscape.

Their conversation then turned to the importance of building trust and alignment between partners, as well as the need for clear communication and shared goals. "Successful partnerships require transparency, open communication, and a shared vision for the future," Sarah emphasized. "By working together as equals and focusing on delivering value for customers, traditional banks and neobanks can create powerful alliances that drive positive change in the industry."

As the roundtable discussion came to a close, Michael left the conference room feeling inspired by Sarah's insights and the potential for partnerships to drive innovation and collaboration in the banking industry. He realized that traditional banks and neobanks were not just competitors; they were partners on a shared journey towards a more inclusive, customer-centric financial ecosystem.

Armed with Sarah's insights, Michael was eager to explore opportunities for partnerships and collaborations between traditional banks and neobanks, knowing that they held the key to unlocking new opportunities and driving positive change in the financial industry and beyond.

## 5.6: Regulatory Considerations for Neobanks

In the heart of Washington D.C., Michael Sawyer found himself in a high-level meeting room at the Federal Reserve, surrounded by regulators and executives from leading neobanks and traditional banks. He had arranged to attend a regulatory summit on the challenges and considerations for neobanks in navigating the complex regulatory landscape.

The room buzzed with anticipation as Rachel Johnson, a senior regulator, took the stage to address the audience. "Good morning, everyone. Today, we're going to discuss the regulatory considerations for neobanks and explore how regulators and industry stakeholders can work together to ensure the safety and soundness of the financial system."

Rachel began by acknowledging the rapid growth of neobanks and the need for regulators to adapt to the evolving banking landscape. "Neobanks have emerged as innovative alternatives to traditional banks, offering customers convenient, digital-first banking experiences," she explained. "However, with innovation comes risk, and it's essential for regulators to strike the right balance between fostering innovation and protecting consumers and the integrity of the financial system."

Michael listened intently as Rachel outlined the key regulatory challenges facing neobanks, including compliance with anti-money laundering (AML) and know-your-customer (KYC) regulations, cybersecurity requirements, and consumer protection laws. He realized that while neobanks offered exciting opportunities for innovation and financial inclusion, they also faced unique regulatory hurdles that required careful navigation and compliance.

Their conversation then turned to the importance of collaboration between regulators, neobanks, and other industry stakeholders to address regulatory challenges and promote responsible innovation. "Regulators play a crucial role in ensuring the safety and stability of the financial system," Rachel emphasized. "By engaging in dialogue with neobanks and other fintech firms, regulators can gain a better understanding of emerging risks and trends and develop tailored regulatory frameworks that foster innovation while safeguarding consumers and the broader economy."

As the summit drew to a close, Michael left the Federal Reserve feeling inspired by Rachel's insights and the commitment of regulators to support responsible innovation in the banking industry. He realized that while regulatory compliance posed challenges for neobanks, it also presented opportunities for collaboration and dialogue between regulators and industry stakeholders.

Armed with Rachel's insights, Michael was eager to explore how neobanks could navigate the regulatory landscape effectively and responsibly, knowing that regulatory compliance was essential for building trust, credibility, and long-term success in the financial industry.

# 6

# Chapter 6: AI and Automation in Banking Operations

## 6.1: AI Applications in Banking

In the heart of a bustling financial district, Michael Sawyer found himself in a state-of-the-art innovation lab at a leading bank, surrounded by cutting-edge technology and a team of brilliant engineers. He had arranged to meet with Dr. Emily Chen, the head of AI research and development, to delve into the transformative impact of artificial intelligence (AI) on banking operations.

Dr. Chen greeted Michael with a warm smile, her enthusiasm for AI palpable as they settled into a cozy meeting area.

"Michael, it's great to have you here," Dr. Chen said, pouring them both cups of freshly brewed coffee. "Let's explore how AI is revolutionizing banking and reshaping the future of financial services."

She began by explaining how AI was being applied across various aspects of banking operations, from customer service and risk management to fraud detection and personalized financial advice. "AI has the potential to enhance efficiency, accuracy, and decision-making in banking," Dr. Chen explained. "By leveraging advanced algorithms and machine learning techniques, banks can automate routine tasks, analyze vast amounts of data, and extract valuable insights to drive better outcomes for customers and the business."

Michael listened intently as Dr. Chen detailed some of the most promising AI applications in banking, including chatbots and virtual assistants for customer support, predictive analytics for credit scoring and loan underwriting, and anomaly detection algorithms for fraud prevention. He realized that AI was not just a buzzword; it was a powerful tool that was transforming the way banks operated and interacted with customers.

Their conversation then turned to the potential challenges and considerations associated with AI adoption in banking, such as data privacy and security concerns, algorithmic bias, and regulatory compliance. "While AI offers tremendous opportunities for innovation and efficiency gains, it also raises important ethical and regulatory questions that must be addressed," Dr. Chen emphasized. "Banks must ensure transparency, accountability, and fairness in their use of AI to maintain trust and credibility with customers and regulators."

As the meeting drew to a close, Michael left the innovation lab feeling inspired by Dr. Chen's insights and the transformative potential of AI in banking. He realized that AI was not just a technology; it was a catalyst for change that was revolutionizing banking operations and driving the industry towards a more efficient, intelligent, and customer-centric future.

Armed with Dr. Chen's insights, Michael was eager to continue his exploration of AI in banking, knowing that it held the key to unlocking new opportunities and driving positive change in the financial industry and beyond.

## 6.2: Chatbots and Virtual Assistants

In a sleek, modern office space adorned with state-of-the-art technology, Michael Sawyer found himself in a demonstration room at a leading fintech company, surrounded by engineers and designers. He had arranged to meet with Sophia Reynolds, the lead developer behind the company's innovative chatbot platform, to explore how chatbots and virtual assistants were reshaping the landscape of banking operations.

Sophia greeted Michael with a warm smile, her excitement for the project evident as they settled into comfortable chairs.

"Michael, it's a pleasure to have you here," Sophia said, gesturing towards the large screen displaying the chatbot interface. "Let me show you how our chatbot is revolutionizing customer interactions in the banking industry."

She began by explaining how the chatbot, named Luna, was designed to assist customers with a wide range of banking tasks, from checking account balances and transferring funds to answering frequently asked questions and providing personalized financial advice. "Luna uses natural language processing and machine learning algorithms to understand and respond to customer queries in real-time," Sophia explained. "She can handle simple inquiries independently and seamlessly escalate more complex issues to human agents when needed."

Michael watched in awe as Sophia demonstrated Luna's capabilities, interacting with the chatbot through a series of questions and commands. He was impressed by Luna's intelligence and responsiveness, as well as her ability to anticipate his needs and provide relevant information and recommendations.

Their conversation then turned to the broader impact of chatbots and virtual assistants on banking operations, including their potential to enhance efficiency, reduce costs, and improve customer satisfaction. "Chatbots and virtual assistants offer a scalable, cost-effective solution for banks to provide personalized, round-the-clock customer support," Sophia remarked. "They can handle a high volume of inquiries simultaneously, freeing up human agents to focus on more complex tasks and delivering a superior customer experience."

As the demonstration came to a close, Michael left the fintech company feeling inspired by Sophia's insights and the potential of chatbots and virtual assistants to transform banking operations. He realized that chatbots were not just tools for automation; they were intelligent assistants that were redefining the way banks interacted with customers and delivering value in ways previously unimaginable.

Armed with Sophia's insights, Michael was eager to explore how chatbots and virtual assistants could be leveraged to enhance customer service, streamline operations, and drive innovation in the banking industry, knowing that they held the key to unlocking new opportunities and delivering exceptional experiences for customers.

## 6.3: Risk Management and Fraud Detection

In a dimly lit conference room at a leading financial institution, Michael Sawyer found himself surrounded by a team of analysts and data scientists, all focused intently on their computer screens. He had arranged to meet with Dr. Alex Nguyen, the head of AI-driven risk management, to uncover how artificial intelligence (AI) was transforming the landscape of risk management and fraud detection in banking operations.

Dr. Nguyen greeted Michael with a firm handshake, his dedication to the task evident in the intensity of his gaze.

"Michael, thank you for joining us," Dr. Nguyen said, gesturing towards the large screen displaying a complex network of data points and transactions. "Let me show you how AI is revolutionizing our approach to risk management and fraud detection."

He began by explaining how the bank had developed an AI-driven system that analyzed vast amounts of transaction data in real-time to identify suspicious patterns and detect potential fraud. "Our AI algorithms use machine learning techniques to continuously learn and adapt to new threats, allowing us to stay one step ahead of fraudsters," Dr. Nguyen explained. "By automating the detection process, we're able to identify and mitigate risks more effectively and efficiently than ever before."

Michael watched in awe as Dr. Nguyen demonstrated the AI system in action, highlighting how it flagged unusual transactions, detected anomalies in customer behavior, and generated alerts for further investigation. He was impressed by the system's speed and accuracy, as well as its ability to detect sophisticated fraud schemes that would have gone unnoticed by traditional methods.

Their conversation then turned to the broader impact of AI on risk management and fraud detection in banking operations, including its potential to reduce losses, protect customer assets, and preserve trust in the financial system. "AI is a game-changer for risk management," Dr. Nguyen remarked. "It enables us to analyze data at scale, identify emerging threats in real-time, and take proactive measures to protect our customers and the bank."

As the demonstration came to a close, Michael left the conference room feeling inspired by Dr. Nguyen's insights and the potential of AI to revolutionize risk management and fraud detection in banking operations. He realized that AI was not just a tool for automation; it was a powerful ally in the fight against financial crime and fraud.

Armed with Dr. Nguyen's insights, Michael was eager to explore how AI could be further leveraged to enhance risk management practices, strengthen cybersecurity measures, and safeguard the integrity of the financial system, knowing that it held the key to unlocking new opportunities and mitigating risks in the banking industry and beyond.

## 6.4: Process Automation and Efficiency Gains

In a sleek, modern office space at the headquarters of a leading bank, Michael Sawyer found himself in a bustling operations center, surrounded by a team of process engineers and automation specialists. He had arranged to meet with Sarah Thompson, the head of process automation, to explore how artificial intelligence (AI) was revolutionizing banking operations and driving efficiency gains through automation.

## CHAPTER 6: AI AND AUTOMATION IN BANKING OPERATIONS

Sarah greeted Michael with a warm smile, her enthusiasm for automation palpable as they settled into a conference room overlooking the bustling trading floor.

"Michael, it's great to have you here," Sarah said, gesturing towards the rows of monitors displaying real-time data and analytics. "Let me show you how AI is transforming our approach to process automation and driving efficiency gains across the bank."

She began by explaining how the bank had implemented AI-driven automation solutions to streamline a wide range of processes, from account opening and loan processing to regulatory reporting and compliance checks. "Our AI algorithms analyze historical data and user interactions to identify repetitive tasks and bottlenecks that can be automated," Sarah explained. "By automating routine processes, we're able to free up human resources, reduce operational costs, and improve overall efficiency."

Michael watched in fascination as Sarah demonstrated the AI-driven automation platform in action, highlighting how it seamlessly integrated with existing systems and workflows to automate manual tasks, reduce processing times, and enhance decision-making capabilities. He was impressed by the platform's versatility and scalability, as well as its ability to adapt to changing business needs and regulatory requirements.

Their conversation then turned to the broader impact of AI-driven process automation on banking operations, including its potential to improve accuracy, reduce errors, and enhance the overall customer experience. "AI-driven process automation is a game-changer for banking operations," Sarah remarked. "It enables us to streamline workflows, eliminate inefficiencies, and deliver faster, more personalized services to our customers."

As the demonstration came to a close, Michael left the operations center feeling inspired by Sarah's insights and the transformative potential of AI-driven process automation in banking operations. He realized that AI was not just a tool for automation; it was a catalyst for innovation that was reshaping the future of banking and driving efficiency gains across the industry.

Armed with Sarah's insights, Michael was eager to explore how AI-driven process automation could be further leveraged to optimize operations, reduce costs, and deliver superior value to customers, knowing that it held the key to unlocking new opportunities and driving sustainable growth in the banking industry and beyond.

## 6.5 Challenges of AI Implementation in Banking

Michael adjusted his tie as he prepared to address a room full of banking executives and AI specialists in London. His previous discussions on AI's potential had sparked enthusiasm, but now it was time to delve into the complexities and hurdles that accompanied its implementation in banking.

### *The Data Quality Conundrum*

In the bustling office of a major London bank, Sarah, the head of AI initiatives, was grappling with a familiar problem. Her team had developed a sophisticated AI model to predict customer churn, but the results were inconsistent.

"Why are we seeing such a high error rate?" Sarah asked, frustration evident in her voice.

"We believe it's the data," her lead data scientist, John, replied. "The historical data we're using is incomplete and inconsistent. Missing values and outdated records are skewing the results."

Sarah knew that for AI to be effective, it required high-quality data. "We need to clean and standardize our data before we can trust these models. Let's focus on improving our data governance practices."

The scene underscored a fundamental challenge in AI implementation: the need for reliable, high-quality data. Without it, even the most advanced AI algorithms could produce flawed results, leading to poor decision-making and eroding trust in the technology.

## *Integration with Legacy Systems*

Meanwhile, in New York, Robert, the CTO of another leading bank, faced a different challenge. His team was struggling to integrate AI tools with the bank's outdated legacy systems.

"The AI solution works perfectly in isolation, but when we try to integrate it with our core banking systems, it crashes," explained Maria, his lead engineer.

Robert sighed. "These legacy systems weren't designed to handle the volume and complexity of data that AI requires. We need a hybrid approach, gradually modernizing our infrastructure while deploying AI."

The scene highlighted the difficulties of integrating cutting-edge AI technologies with legacy systems, a common hurdle for many traditional banks. Achieving seamless integration required significant investment in both time and resources, as well as strategic planning to ensure continuity and minimal disruption.

## Ethical and Bias Concerns

In a conference room in San Francisco, Lisa, an AI ethics consultant, was leading a workshop for a group of bankers. She presented a case study where an AI loan approval system had inadvertently discriminated against certain demographic groups.

"This system, trained on historical data, learned biases present in the data," Lisa explained. "As a result, it unfairly denied loans to minority applicants."

Michael, attending the workshop, nodded thoughtfully. "We must ensure our AI systems are transparent and fair. How can we identify and mitigate these biases?"

Lisa responded, "It starts with diverse and unbiased training data, continuous monitoring, and involving ethicists in the development process. We must also be transparent with our customers about how AI decisions are made."

The discussion emphasized the ethical challenges of AI in banking. Ensuring fairness and transparency was crucial to maintaining customer trust and adhering to regulatory standards.

## Skills Gap and Change Management

Back in London, Michael met with Claire, the bank's HR director, to discuss another pressing issue: the skills gap. As the bank adopted more AI-driven processes, the need for employees with AI expertise became critical.

"We're facing a significant skills shortage," Claire admitted. "Our current staff lacks the necessary AI and data science skills, and finding qualified candidates is challenging."

Michael suggested, "We need to invest in training programs for our existing employees and collaborate with universities to develop a pipeline of talent."

The scene highlighted the human resources challenge of AI implementation. Bridging the skills gap required strategic initiatives to upskill current employees and attract new talent, ensuring the bank could effectively leverage AI technologies.

## *Regulatory and Compliance Issues*

In Brussels, a meeting was underway between regulators and banking representatives. Isabelle, a compliance officer from a prominent bank, voiced her concerns about AI regulations.

"AI is evolving rapidly, but our regulatory frameworks are lagging. We need clear guidelines to ensure our AI applications comply with existing laws," she stated.

A regulator responded, "We understand the need for clarity. We're working on developing comprehensive AI regulations, but it's a complex process. In the meantime, we encourage banks to adhere to best practices and self-regulate."

The conversation underscored the regulatory challenges of AI in banking. As regulations struggled to keep pace with technological advancements, banks had to navigate a landscape of uncertainty, balancing innovation with compliance.

## *The Path Forward*

Michael concluded his session in London by addressing the audience. "AI holds immense potential to transform banking, but its implementation is fraught with challenges. From data quality and integration issues to ethical concerns and regulatory hurdles, we must approach AI with a strategic, responsible mindset."

He continued, "By investing in data governance, modernizing our infrastructure, fostering ethical AI practices, bridging the skills gap, and collaborating with regulators, we can overcome these challenges. Together, we can harness the power of AI to create a more efficient, inclusive, and innovative banking industry."

As the audience applauded, Michael felt a sense of resolve. The journey to AI-driven banking was complex, but with careful planning and collaboration, the future of finance could indeed be reinvented.

## 6.6: Ethical Considerations and Future Outlook

In a serene boardroom at the headquarters of a leading bank, Michael Sawyer found himself in the midst of a heated discussion, surrounded by executives and experts from various fields. He had arranged to attend a forum on the ethical considerations surrounding the implementation of artificial intelligence (AI) in banking operations, led by Dr. Elena Martinez, a renowned ethicist.

Dr. Martinez greeted Michael with a nod, her demeanor poised and thoughtful as they settled around the polished wooden table.

"Michael, thank you for joining us," Dr. Martinez said, her gaze sweeping across the room. "Let's delve into the ethical considerations surrounding the implementation of AI in banking operations and explore the path forward."

She began by acknowledging the transformative potential of AI in banking, from enhancing customer service to streamlining operations and reducing costs. "AI has the power to revolutionize banking operations, but it also raises important ethical questions that must be addressed," Dr. Martinez explained. "From concerns about data privacy and algorithmic bias to questions of accountability and transparency, banks must navigate a complex ethical landscape to ensure that AI is deployed responsibly and ethically."

Michael listened intently as Dr. Martinez highlighted some of the key ethical challenges facing banks in the implementation of AI, including the potential for discrimination and bias in algorithmic decision-making, the risk of data breaches and privacy violations, and the need for transparency and accountability in AI systems. He realized that while AI offered tremendous opportunities for innovation and efficiency gains, it also posed significant ethical risks that required careful consideration and mitigation.

Their discussion then turned to the future outlook for AI in banking and the steps that banks could take to ensure that AI was deployed in a way that was ethical, responsible, and aligned with the interests of customers and society as a whole. "As banks continue to invest in AI and automation, it's essential that they prioritize ethics and values in their decision-making processes," Dr. Martinez emphasized. "By embedding ethical considerations into the design, development, and deployment of AI systems, banks can build trust, credibility, and long-term success in the digital age."

As the forum drew to a close, Michael left the boardroom feeling inspired by Dr. Martinez's insights and the commitment of banks to ethical AI implementation. He realized that while AI offered exciting opportunities for innovation and growth, it also required careful stewardship and ethical leadership to ensure that its benefits were shared equitably and its risks were mitigated responsibly.

Armed with Dr. Martinez's insights, Michael was eager to continue his exploration of AI in banking, knowing that ethical considerations would play a critical role in shaping the future of the industry and its relationship with technology.

# 7

# Chapter 7: Financial Inclusion and Access

## 7.1: The Importance of Financial Inclusion

In a bustling community center nestled in the heart of a vibrant city, Michael Sawyer found himself surrounded by a diverse group of individuals, all eager to participate in a workshop on financial inclusion and access. He had arranged to attend the event, led by Maria Garcia, a passionate advocate for financial empowerment.

Maria greeted Michael with a warm smile, her enthusiasm for the topic evident in her welcoming demeanor.

"Michael, welcome to our workshop on financial inclusion," Maria said, gesturing towards the gathered participants. "Today, we're going to explore why financial inclusion is so important and discuss strategies for expanding access to financial services for all."

She began by highlighting the significance of financial inclusion in promoting economic stability, reducing poverty, and fostering social development. "Financial inclusion is not just about access to bank accounts and credit," Maria explained. "It's about empowering individuals and communities to build a better future for themselves and their families, regardless of their socio-economic status or background."

Michael listened intently as Maria shared stories of individuals who had been excluded from the financial system and the impact it had on their lives. From immigrants struggling to send remittances to their families abroad to small business owners unable to access credit to grow their businesses, the barriers to financial inclusion were vast and varied.

Their discussion then turned to the role of technology in expanding access to financial services and empowering underserved communities. "Technology has the power to break down barriers and democratize access to financial services," Maria remarked. "From mobile banking apps to digital payment platforms, technology is revolutionizing the way we bank and opening up new opportunities for financial inclusion."

As the workshop came to a close, Michael left the community center feeling inspired by Maria's passion and the collective commitment of the participants to drive positive change in their communities. He realized that financial inclusion was not just a goal to strive for; it was a fundamental human right that required the collective effort of governments, financial institutions, and civil society to achieve.

Armed with Maria's insights, Michael was eager to continue his advocacy for financial inclusion and access, knowing that it held the key to unlocking new opportunities and building a more inclusive and equitable society for all.

## 7.2: Technology Solutions for Financial Inclusion

In a bustling co-working space buzzing with energy, Michael Sawyer found himself surrounded by a group of entrepreneurs and innovators, all gathered for a hackathon focused on developing technology solutions for financial inclusion. He had arranged to participate in the event, led by Dr. Sanjay Patel, a visionary technologist dedicated to harnessing the power of technology for social good.

Dr. Patel greeted Michael with a firm handshake, his excitement for the hackathon evident in his enthusiastic demeanor.

"Michael, welcome to our hackathon on technology solutions for financial inclusion," Dr. Patel said, gesturing towards the rows of laptops and whiteboards adorned with brainstorming ideas. "Today, we're going to leverage the power of technology to break down barriers and expand access to financial services for all."

He began by outlining the challenges faced by underserved communities in accessing traditional banking services and the transformative potential of technology in addressing these challenges. "Technology has the power to revolutionize the way we bank and empower individuals and communities to take control of their financial futures," Dr. Patel explained. "From mobile banking apps to digital payment platforms to blockchain-based solutions, there are countless opportunities to leverage technology for financial inclusion."

Michael listened intently as Dr. Patel shared examples of technology solutions that were already making a difference in the lives of underserved populations around the world. From mobile money platforms that enabled individuals to send and receive payments using their smartphones to peer-to-peer lending networks that connected borrowers with investors online, the possibilities were endless.

Their discussion then turned to the hackathon itself, with participants forming teams and brainstorming ideas for innovative technology solutions to address specific challenges faced by underserved communities. Armed with laptops and whiteboards, they set to work, collaborating and iterating on their ideas with enthusiasm and determination.

As the hackathon progressed, Michael was struck by the creativity and ingenuity of the participants, as well as their unwavering commitment to using technology for social good. He realized that by harnessing the power of technology and collective action, they had the potential to drive meaningful change and create a more inclusive and equitable financial system for all.

Armed with Dr. Patel's insights, Michael was eager to continue his exploration of technology solutions for financial inclusion, knowing that they held the key to unlocking new opportunities and building a more inclusive and prosperous future for communities around the world.

## 7.3: Banking the Unbanked: Initiatives and Challenges

In a humble community center nestled in a rural village, Michael Sawyer found himself surrounded by a group of local leaders and activists, all gathered for a town hall meeting on banking the unbanked. He had arranged to attend the event, led by Maria Lopez, a tireless advocate for financial empowerment in underserved communities.

Maria welcomed Michael with a warm embrace, her determination to make a difference evident in her compassionate gaze.

"Michael, thank you for joining us," Maria said, gesturing towards the gathered crowd. "Today, we're going to discuss initiatives to bank the unbanked and the challenges we face in bringing financial services to underserved communities."

She began by highlighting the importance of banking the unbanked in promoting economic empowerment, reducing poverty, and fostering social inclusion. "For too long, underserved communities have been left behind by the traditional banking system," Maria explained. "But by working together, we can break down barriers and create opportunities for everyone to access the financial tools they need to build a better future."

Michael listened intently as Maria shared stories of individuals in the community who had been excluded from the financial system and the impact it had on their lives. From farmers unable to access credit to entrepreneurs struggling to save for the future, the challenges faced by the unbanked were vast and varied.

Their discussion then turned to the initiatives underway to bank the unbanked, from community-based credit unions to mobile banking solutions to financial literacy programs. "We're seeing incredible innovation and creativity in our efforts to bring financial services to underserved communities," Maria remarked. "But we also face significant challenges, from limited infrastructure and resources to cultural barriers and trust issues."

As the town hall meeting came to a close, Michael left the community center feeling inspired by Maria's leadership and the collective determination of the community to overcome challenges and create a more inclusive and equitable financial system for all. He realized that banking the unbanked was not just a goal to strive for; it was a fundamental human right that required the collective effort of governments, financial institutions, and civil society to achieve.

Armed with Maria's insights, Michael was eager to continue his advocacy for financial inclusion and access, knowing that it held the key to unlocking new opportunities and building a brighter future for underserved communities around the world.

## 7.4: Microfinance and Alternative Banking Models

In a bustling marketplace teeming with life and activity, Michael Sawyer found himself in the heart of a community transformed by the power of microfinance. He had arranged to visit the marketplace, led by Sofia Rahman, a pioneering microfinance entrepreneur dedicated to empowering women and small business owners in underserved communities.

Sofia welcomed Michael with a warm smile, her passion for microfinance evident in her vibrant presence.

"Michael, I'm thrilled to have you here," Sofia said, gesturing towards the bustling stalls and vendors. "Today, I want to show you how microfinance and alternative banking models are transforming the lives of individuals and communities."

She began by explaining the concept of microfinance and its role in providing financial services to those traditionally excluded from the formal banking sector. "Microfinance is about more than just providing loans; it's about empowering individuals to lift themselves out of poverty and build a better future for themselves and their families," Sofia explained. "By offering small loans, savings accounts, and financial education, microfinance institutions are helping entrepreneurs and small business owners to start and grow their businesses, create jobs, and improve their standard of living."

Michael listened intently as Sofia shared stories of women who had used microloans to start their own businesses, farmers who had accessed credit to invest in their crops, and artisans who had saved money to send their children to school. The impact of microfinance on the community was tangible, with businesses thriving, families prospering, and hope blossoming in every corner of the marketplace.

Their conversation then turned to alternative banking models, from community-based credit unions to digital lending platforms to peer-to-peer lending networks. "Alternative banking models are democratizing access to financial services and empowering individuals to take control of their financial futures," Sofia remarked. "By leveraging technology and community networks, these models are breaking down barriers and creating opportunities for financial inclusion where none existed before."

As they strolled through the marketplace, Michael witnessed firsthand the transformative power of microfinance and alternative banking models in action. He realized that by providing access to financial services and fostering entrepreneurship, these models were not just changing lives; they were building stronger, more resilient communities for generations to come.

Armed with Sofia's insights, Michael was inspired to continue his support for microfinance and alternative banking models, knowing that they held the key to unlocking new opportunities and driving sustainable development in underserved communities around the world.

## 7.5: Partnerships for Inclusive Banking

In a bustling conference room adorned with banners of various organizations, Michael Sawyer found himself amidst a gathering of industry leaders and advocates for financial inclusion. He had arranged to attend a summit focused on partnerships for inclusive banking, led by Sarah Johnson, a seasoned strategist renowned for her collaborative approach to driving social change.

Sarah greeted Michael with a firm handshake, her determination to foster collaboration evident in her warm smile.

"Michael, it's wonderful to have you join us," Sarah said, gesturing towards the diverse group of attendees. "Today, we're here to explore the power of partnerships in advancing financial inclusion and creating a more equitable banking system for all."

She began by emphasizing the importance of collaboration in tackling the complex challenges of financial exclusion. "No single organization or sector can solve the problem of financial exclusion alone," Sarah explained. "By working together across sectors and leveraging each other's strengths, we can create innovative solutions and drive meaningful change that benefits everyone."

Michael listened intently as Sarah shared examples of successful partnerships for inclusive banking, from collaborations between banks and non-profit organizations to public-private partnerships with governments and international agencies. "Partnerships allow us to pool resources, share knowledge, and scale impact in ways that would be impossible on our own," Sarah remarked. "By partnering with diverse stakeholders, we can reach more underserved communities, tailor solutions to their unique needs, and create lasting change that extends far beyond our individual efforts."

Their discussion then turned to the keys to successful partnerships for inclusive banking, including clear communication, shared goals and values, and mutual respect and trust. "Building effective partnerships requires time, effort, and commitment from all parties involved," Sarah emphasized. "But the rewards are immense, as we see the impact of our collective efforts in the lives of individuals and communities around the world."

As the summit progressed, Michael was struck by the spirit of collaboration and camaraderie in the room, as leaders from different sectors came together to brainstorm ideas, share best practices, and forge new partnerships for inclusive banking. He realized that by working together, they had the potential to create a more inclusive and equitable banking system that served the needs of all people, regardless of their socio-economic status or background.

Armed with Sarah's insights, Michael was inspired to continue his advocacy for partnerships for inclusive banking, knowing that they held the key to unlocking new opportunities and building a brighter future for communities around the world.

## 7.6: Measuring Success: Impact Metrics and Case Studies

In a sleek conference room filled with charts and graphs, Michael Sawyer found himself among a group of analysts and researchers gathered for a symposium on measuring success in financial inclusion initiatives. He had arranged to attend the event, led by Dr. Emily Chen, a leading expert in impact evaluation and measurement.

Dr. Chen greeted Michael with a warm smile, her passion for data-driven insights evident in her welcoming demeanor.

"Michael, I'm delighted to have you join us," Dr. Chen said, gesturing towards the rows of analysts and researchers. "Today, we're here to discuss how we can effectively measure the impact of financial inclusion initiatives and learn from case studies of successful programs around the world."

She began by emphasizing the importance of impact measurement in ensuring accountability, driving informed decision-making, and maximizing the effectiveness of financial inclusion efforts. "Measuring success is critical in our journey towards financial inclusion," Dr. Chen explained. "It allows us to understand what works, what doesn't, and how we can improve our strategies to better serve the needs of underserved communities."

Michael listened intently as Dr. Chen shared insights into key impact metrics for financial inclusion initiatives, including access to financial services, usage of financial products, and improvements in socio-economic outcomes. "By tracking these metrics over time, we can assess the effectiveness of our interventions and identify areas for improvement," Dr. Chen remarked. "But impact measurement is not just about numbers; it's also about understanding the stories behind the data and the real-world impact of our work on the lives of individuals and communities."

Their discussion then turned to case studies of successful financial inclusion programs from around the world, ranging from mobile banking initiatives in sub-Saharan Africa to microfinance programs in South Asia to community-based credit unions in Latin America. "These case studies provide valuable insights into what works in financial inclusion and the factors that contribute to success," Dr. Chen explained. "By learning from these examples, we can identify best practices, replicate successful strategies, and drive greater impact in our own initiatives."

As the symposium came to a close, Michael left the conference room feeling inspired by Dr. Chen's insights and the collective commitment of the analysts and researchers to drive progress in financial inclusion. He realized that by effectively measuring success and learning from case studies of successful programs, they had the potential to accelerate progress towards a more inclusive and equitable financial system for all.

Armed with Dr. Chen's insights, Michael was eager to continue his work in financial inclusion, knowing that impact measurement held the key to unlocking new opportunities and driving meaningful change in underserved communities around the world.

# 8

# Chapter 8: Sustainability and Responsible Banking

8.1: The Role of Banks in Sustainable Development

In a serene boardroom adorned with greenery and natural light, Michael Sawyer found himself among a group of executives and sustainability experts gathered for a symposium on responsible banking. He had arranged to attend the event, led by Dr. Elena Fernandez, a leading advocate for sustainable development in the banking sector.

Dr. Fernandez welcomed Michael with a warm smile, her passion for responsible banking evident in her graceful demeanor.

"Michael, it's wonderful to have you join us," Dr. Fernandez said, gesturing towards the panoramic view of the city skyline. "Today, we're here to explore the role of banks in driving sustainable development and creating positive social and environmental impact."

She began by emphasizing the importance of responsible

banking in addressing pressing global challenges, from climate change to income inequality to social injustice. "Banks play a pivotal role in shaping the future of our planet and society," Dr. Fernandez explained. "By integrating environmental, social, and governance (ESG) criteria into their operations and decision-making processes, banks can drive positive change and contribute to a more sustainable and equitable world."

Michael listened intently as Dr. Fernandez shared insights into the ways in which banks could promote sustainable development, from financing renewable energy projects to supporting small and medium-sized enterprises (SMEs) to promoting financial literacy and inclusion. "Responsible banking is not just about minimizing harm; it's about maximizing positive impact," Dr. Fernandez remarked. "By aligning their business practices with the principles of sustainability, banks can create value for their shareholders, customers, and society as a whole."

Their discussion then turned to case studies of banks that had successfully integrated sustainability into their business models and operations. From green bond issuances to community investment programs to carbon footprint reduction initiatives, these case studies showcased the diverse ways in which banks could drive positive change and contribute to sustainable development.

As the symposium came to a close, Michael left the boardroom feeling inspired by Dr. Fernandez's insights and the collective commitment of the executives and experts to responsible banking. He realized that by embracing sustainability and responsible practices, banks had the power to be agents of positive change and drive meaningful progress towards a more sustainable and equitable future for all.

Armed with Dr. Fernandez's insights, Michael was eager to continue his advocacy for responsible banking, knowing that it held the key to unlocking new opportunities and building a better tomorrow for generations to come.

## 8.2: Environmental, Social, and Governance (ESG) Criteria

In a modern conference room adorned with sustainability-themed artwork, Michael Sawyer found himself among a group of bankers and sustainability experts gathered for a seminar on ESG criteria in banking. He had arranged to attend the event, led by Professor Emma Carter, a renowned expert in sustainable finance.

Professor Carter greeted Michael with a warm smile, her passion for ESG integration evident in her welcoming demeanor.

"Michael, I'm delighted to have you join us," Professor Carter said, gesturing towards the interactive screens displaying ESG data. "Today, we're here to delve into the importance of environmental, social, and governance criteria in shaping responsible banking practices."

She began by explaining the significance of ESG criteria in evaluating the sustainability and ethical impact of investments and business operations. "ESG criteria provide a framework for assessing a company's performance across key sustainability dimensions," Professor Carter explained. "By considering factors such as carbon emissions, labor practices, diversity and inclusion, and board governance, banks can make more informed decisions that drive positive social and environmental outcomes."

Michael listened intently as Professor Carter shared insights into the ways in which banks could incorporate ESG criteria into their risk management, investment decision-making, and stakeholder engagement processes. "ESG integration is not just about compliance; it's about creating long-term value for all stakeholders," Professor Carter remarked. "By identifying and mitigating ESG risks and seizing ESG-related opportunities, banks can enhance their financial performance, mitigate reputational risks, and contribute to a more sustainable and resilient economy."

Their discussion then turned to case studies of banks that had successfully integrated ESG criteria into their business practices and investment strategies. From sustainable lending programs to impact investing portfolios to ESG-focused shareholder engagement initiatives, these case studies showcased the diverse ways in which banks could leverage ESG criteria to drive positive change and create shared value.

As the seminar came to a close, Michael left the conference room feeling inspired by Professor Carter's insights and the collective commitment of the bankers and experts to ESG integration in banking. He realized that by embracing ESG criteria, banks had the power to align their operations with the principles of sustainability and responsibility, and drive meaningful progress towards a more inclusive, equitable, and sustainable future for all.

Armed with Professor Carter's insights, Michael was eager to continue his advocacy for ESG integration in banking, knowing that it held the key to unlocking new opportunities and building a better tomorrow for generations to come.

## 8.3: Green Finance and Climate Action

In a conference hall adorned with images of lush forests and renewable energy projects, Michael Sawyer found himself among a group of financiers and environmentalists gathered for a summit on green finance and climate action. He had arranged to attend the event, led by Dr. Maya Patel, a leading advocate for sustainable investment and climate resilience.

Dr. Patel welcomed Michael with a firm handshake, her passion for environmental stewardship evident in her determined gaze.

"Michael, it's a pleasure to have you join us," Dr. Patel said, gesturing towards the panoramic backdrop of wind turbines and solar panels. "Today, we're here to explore the critical role of green finance in combating climate change and building a more sustainable future for our planet."

She began by emphasizing the urgency of the climate crisis and the need for bold action from the financial sector. "Climate change is the defining challenge of our time, and the financial sector has a crucial role to play in addressing it," Dr. Patel explained. "By mobilizing capital towards low-carbon, climate-resilient investments, banks can drive the transition to a sustainable, low-carbon economy and help mitigate the worst impacts of climate change."

Michael listened intently as Dr. Patel shared insights into the ways in which banks could support climate action through green finance initiatives, such as renewable energy financing, green bonds, and sustainable infrastructure investments. "Green finance is not just about protecting the environment; it's also about creating economic opportunities, fostering innovation, and building resilience to climate risks," Dr. Patel remarked. "By channeling capital towards climate-friendly projects and businesses, banks can generate positive environmental and social impact while also delivering financial returns for their investors."

Their discussion then turned to case studies of banks that had successfully implemented green finance initiatives and supported climate action. From financing solar farms to funding energy efficiency retrofits to underwriting climate resilience projects, these case studies showcased the diverse ways in which banks could leverage green finance to drive positive change and contribute to a more sustainable future.

As the summit came to a close, Michael left the conference hall feeling inspired by Dr. Patel's insights and the collective commitment of the financiers and environmentalists to green finance and climate action. He realized that by embracing green finance, banks had the power to be catalysts for change and leaders in the fight against climate change.

Armed with Dr. Patel's insights, Michael was eager to continue his advocacy for green finance and climate action, knowing that they held the key to unlocking new opportunities and building a more sustainable future for generations to come.

## 8.4: Social Impact Investing and Community Development

In a vibrant community center buzzing with energy and enthusiasm, Michael Sawyer found himself among a diverse group of investors and community leaders gathered for a forum on social impact investing and community development. He had arranged to attend the event, led by Dr. Sophia Nguyen, a passionate advocate for leveraging finance to address social and economic challenges.

Dr. Nguyen greeted Michael with a warm smile, her commitment to empowering communities evident in her welcoming demeanor.

"Michael, it's wonderful to have you join us," Dr. Nguyen said, gesturing towards the bustling room filled with people from all walks of life. "Today, we're here to explore the power of social impact investing in driving positive change and fostering inclusive community development."

She began by emphasizing the importance of investing in projects and businesses that create meaningful social and economic impact in underserved communities. "Social impact investing is about more than just financial returns; it's about generating positive change and improving people's lives," Dr. Nguyen explained. "By directing capital towards initiatives that address pressing social and environmental challenges, banks can play a vital role in building stronger, more resilient communities."

Michael listened intently as Dr. Nguyen shared insights into the ways in which banks could support community development through social impact investing, such as financing affordable housing, supporting small businesses, and investing in education and healthcare initiatives. "Social impact investing enables banks to deploy their resources in ways that benefit society as a whole, while also generating financial returns for their investors," Dr. Nguyen remarked. "It's a win-win proposition that creates value for both investors and communities."

Their discussion then turned to case studies of banks that had successfully implemented social impact investing strategies and supported community development projects. From funding community development financial institutions (CD-FIs) to launching impact investment funds to partnering with local organizations, these case studies showcased the diverse ways in which banks could leverage social impact investing to drive positive change and promote inclusive growth.

As the forum came to a close, Michael left the community center feeling inspired by Dr. Nguyen's insights and the collective commitment of the investors and community leaders to social impact investing and community development. He realized that by embracing social impact investing, banks had the power to be agents of positive change and catalysts for community transformation.

Armed with Dr. Nguyen's insights, Michael was eager to continue his advocacy for social impact investing and community development, knowing that they held the key to unlocking new opportunities and building a more inclusive and equitable society for all.

## 8.5: Challenges and Opportunities for Responsible Banking

In a sleek corporate boardroom adorned with sustainability-themed artwork, Michael Sawyer found himself among a group of banking executives and industry experts gathered for a roundtable discussion on responsible banking. He had arranged to attend the event, led by Mr. David Thompson, a seasoned leader in sustainable finance.

Mr. Thompson welcomed Michael with a firm handshake, his commitment to responsible banking evident in his determined demeanor.

"Michael, it's a pleasure to have you join us," Mr. Thompson said, gesturing towards the panoramic view of the city skyline. "Today, we're here to explore the challenges and opportunities that banks face in their journey towards greater sustainability and responsibility."

He began by acknowledging the complexities and obstacles that banks encounter in integrating sustainability into their business models and operations. "Responsible banking is not without its challenges," Mr. Thompson explained. "From regulatory compliance to stakeholder expectations to balancing financial returns with social and environmental impact, banks must navigate a complex landscape of competing priorities and interests."

Michael listened intently as Mr. Thompson shared insights into the key challenges facing responsible banking, such as aligning business objectives with sustainability goals, managing ESG risks, and measuring impact effectively. "But amidst these challenges, there are also tremendous opportunities for banks to differentiate themselves, drive innovation, and create lasting value for their stakeholders," Mr. Thompson remarked. "By embracing responsible banking practices, banks can enhance their reputation, attract new customers, and build long-term resilience in an increasingly uncertain world."

Their discussion then turned to the opportunities that responsible banking presents, including access to new markets, the potential for product innovation, and the ability to foster deeper relationships with customers and communities. "Responsible banking is not just a moral imperative; it's also a strategic imperative," Mr. Thompson emphasized. "By integrating sustainability into their core business strategies, banks can position themselves for long-term success and contribute to a more sustainable and equitable future."

As the roundtable discussion came to a close, Michael left the boardroom feeling inspired by Mr. Thompson's insights and the collective commitment of the executives and experts to responsible banking. He realized that while the journey towards sustainability may be challenging, it also held the potential to unlock new opportunities and drive meaningful progress towards a more inclusive, resilient, and sustainable banking sector.

Armed with Mr. Thompson's insights, Michael was eager to continue his advocacy for responsible banking, knowing that it held the key to unlocking new opportunities and building a better future for generations to come.

## 8.6: Leading the Change: Best Practices in Responsible Banking

Michael leaned back in his chair, surveying the room filled with the bank's top executives. Today's meeting was pivotal. They were about to embark on a journey to transform their institution into a leader in responsible banking.

### *Setting the Vision*

At the head of the table, Maria, the newly appointed Chief Sustainability Officer, stood up. "We need a vision that aligns our financial success with our responsibility to the planet and society," she began.

Michael nodded, encouraging her to continue. "Our bank has a legacy, but we need to evolve. We must integrate Environmental, Social, and Governance (ESG) criteria into our core operations."

The executives exchanged looks of determination. They knew the path ahead would be challenging, but the urgency of their mission was clear.

## *Building a Sustainable Strategy*

In the weeks that followed, Maria led a series of workshops with various departments. She sat with the risk management team, discussing how to incorporate ESG risks into their models.

"We need to assess not just the financial risks but also the environmental and social risks of our investments," she explained to David, the head of risk management.

David frowned. "That means overhauling our entire risk assessment framework."

"Yes, it does," Maria agreed. "But it's essential for our long-term sustainability."

Meanwhile, Michael worked with the marketing team to craft a campaign that communicated their new commitment to responsible banking. He wanted their customers to see the bank as a force for good.

## *Implementing Green Finance*

One of the bank's flagship initiatives was green finance. They launched a new line of green bonds, specifically designed to fund environmentally sustainable projects.

At the launch event, held at a solar farm funded by one of these bonds, Michael addressed the attendees. "This is just the beginning. Our green bonds will support renewable energy, clean water, and other critical projects that combat climate change."

The media coverage was overwhelmingly positive, and customers began to see the bank not just as a financial institution but as a partner in building a sustainable future.

## *Engaging with the Community*

Another cornerstone of their strategy was community engagement. The bank partnered with local organizations to support financial literacy programs, aimed at underserved communities.

Michael visited a community center in a low-income neighborhood, where a financial literacy workshop was in progress. He watched as a bank employee explained the basics of budgeting to a group of eager participants.

"This is how we make a real impact," Michael said to Maria, who had joined him. "By empowering individuals, we can help build a more inclusive economy."

## *Driving Internal Culture Change*

Transforming the bank's external image was important, but Michael knew that internal culture change was crucial. He and Maria launched a comprehensive training program for all employees, focused on sustainability and ethical banking practices.

At one of the training sessions, Sarah, a young analyst, asked, "How can we ensure that these values are truly integrated into our daily work?"

Maria responded, "It's about making sustainability part of every decision we make. From the projects we fund to the way we operate our offices, every action should reflect our commitment to responsible banking."

## *Measuring Impact and Reporting*

Transparency was key to their strategy. The bank implemented robust systems for measuring and reporting their ESG impacts. They published an annual sustainability report, detailing their progress and areas for improvement.

In a meeting with the board, Michael presented the first report. "We've made significant strides, but we must hold ourselves accountable. This report is not just a document; it's a commitment to continuous improvement."

The board members were impressed by the depth and honesty of the report. It was clear that the bank was serious about its transformation.

## *Leading by Example*

The true test of their efforts came when other banks began to take notice. At an international banking conference, Michael was invited to speak about their journey.

"Leading the change in responsible banking is not easy," he said to the audience of global banking leaders. "It requires a deep commitment to sustainability, transparency, and ethical practices. But the rewards are immense—for our planet, our society, and our businesses."

His speech was met with a standing ovation. It was clear that the bank had not only transformed itself but had also set a new standard for the industry.

## A New Era of Banking

Back in his office, Michael reflected on their journey. The bank had come a long way, but he knew their work was far from over. The path to truly responsible banking was ongoing, requiring constant vigilance and innovation.

Maria joined him, holding a small potted plant. "A gift from one of the community gardens we funded," she said with a smile.

Michael took the plant, feeling a renewed sense of purpose. "It's a symbol of our commitment," he said. "To nurture and grow a better future for everyone."

Together, they looked out over the city skyline, confident that they were leading the change toward a more sustainable and responsible banking industry.

# 9

# Chapter 9: RegTech and Compliance Innovation

## 9.1: Introduction to Regulatory Technology (RegTech)

In a sleek conference room buzzing with anticipation, Michael Sawyer found himself among a group of compliance professionals and technology experts gathered for a seminar on regulatory technology (RegTech). He had arranged to attend the event, led by Ms. Emily Chen, a trailblazer in the field of regulatory innovation.

Ms. Chen welcomed Michael with a bright smile, her enthusiasm for RegTech palpable in her welcoming demeanor.

"Michael, it's fantastic to have you join us," Ms. Chen said, gesturing towards the dynamic presentation screens displaying regulatory frameworks and innovative technologies. "Today, we're here to explore the exciting world of regulatory technology and its transformative potential in the banking sector."

She began by explaining the concept of RegTech and its

## CHAPTER 9: REGTECH AND COMPLIANCE INNOVATION

role in revolutionizing compliance processes and regulatory reporting. "Regulatory technology, or RegTech, refers to the use of advanced technologies such as artificial intelligence, machine learning, and big data analytics to streamline and automate compliance tasks," Ms. Chen explained. "By harnessing the power of technology, banks can enhance regulatory compliance, reduce operational costs, and improve risk management practices."

Michael listened intently as Ms. Chen shared insights into the ways in which RegTech solutions could help banks navigate the increasingly complex and dynamic regulatory landscape. "RegTech offers a wide range of innovative solutions, from automated risk assessments to real-time monitoring to predictive analytics," Ms. Chen remarked. "These technologies enable banks to stay ahead of regulatory requirements, identify potential compliance issues proactively, and make more informed business decisions."

Their discussion then turned to case studies of banks that had successfully implemented RegTech solutions and reaped the benefits of enhanced compliance efficiency and effectiveness. From automated regulatory reporting to AI-powered transaction monitoring to blockchain-based identity verification, these case studies showcased the diverse ways in which RegTech was transforming the compliance function and driving regulatory innovation in the banking industry.

As the seminar came to a close, Michael left the conference room feeling inspired by Ms. Chen's insights and the collective enthusiasm of the compliance professionals and technology experts for RegTech. He realized that by embracing regulatory technology, banks had the opportunity to revolutionize their compliance processes, enhance regulatory compliance, and unlock new opportunities for innovation and growth.

Armed with Ms. Chen's insights, Michael was eager to explore the potential of RegTech further and advocate for its adoption within his organization, knowing that it held the key to navigating the regulatory landscape more effectively and building a more resilient and agile banking sector.

## 9.2: Compliance Challenges in Banking

In a dimly lit boardroom filled with the weight of regulatory documents, Michael Sawyer found himself among a group of compliance officers and legal advisors gathered for a workshop on compliance challenges in banking. Led by Mr. James Richardson, a seasoned expert in regulatory affairs, the session promised to shed light on the complexities of compliance in the banking industry.

Mr. Richardson welcomed Michael with a firm handshake, his demeanor reflecting the seriousness of the topic at hand.

"Michael, I'm glad you could join us," Mr. Richardson said, gesturing towards the towering stack of compliance manuals on the table. "Today, we're here to confront the compliance challenges that banks face in meeting regulatory requirements and maintaining adherence to ever-evolving standards."

He began by outlining the myriad challenges that banks encounter in navigating the intricate web of regulations, from stringent anti-money laundering (AML) laws to complex data privacy regulations to rapidly changing cybersecurity threats. "Compliance in banking is like navigating a labyrinth, with new regulations emerging constantly and regulators increasing their scrutiny," Mr. Richardson explained. "Banks must contend with a host of challenges, including interpreting ambiguous regulations, managing compliance across multiple jurisdictions, and keeping pace with technological advancements."

Michael listened intently as Mr. Richardson shared insights into the specific compliance challenges that banks grapple with on a daily basis, such as conducting thorough customer due diligence, implementing robust risk management frameworks, and ensuring data security and privacy. "Compliance failures can have serious consequences for banks, including hefty fines, reputational damage, and loss of customer trust," Mr. Richardson remarked. "It's imperative for banks to proactively address these challenges and implement effective compliance strategies to mitigate risk and ensure regulatory compliance."

Their discussion then turned to real-life examples of compliance challenges faced by banks, ranging from data breaches to regulatory investigations to enforcement actions. These case studies underscored the importance of proactive compliance management and the need for banks to stay vigilant in the face of evolving regulatory requirements and enforcement priorities.

As the workshop came to a close, Michael left the boardroom feeling sobered by the gravity of the compliance challenges discussed. However, he also felt a renewed sense of determination to address these challenges head-on and leverage innovative solutions such as RegTech to enhance compliance efficiency and effectiveness.

Armed with Mr. Richardson's insights, Michael was ready to confront the compliance maze with confidence, knowing that by proactively addressing compliance challenges, banks could safeguard their reputation, protect their customers, and ensure their long-term success in an increasingly regulated environment.

## 9.3: Automated Compliance Solutions

In a state-of-the-art innovation lab buzzing with the hum of technology, Michael Sawyer found himself among a group of software developers and compliance experts gathered for a demonstration on automated compliance solutions. Led by Dr. Rebecca Evans, a leading figure in RegTech innovation, the session promised to showcase the latest advancements in automating compliance processes.

Dr. Evans greeted Michael with a warm smile, her excitement for technology innovation evident in her enthusiastic demeanor.

"Michael, welcome to our innovation lab," Dr. Evans said, gesturing towards the sleek rows of computer monitors displaying lines of code. "Today, we're here to explore the transformative power of automated compliance solutions in revolutionizing the way banks manage regulatory compliance."

She began by explaining the concept of automated compliance solutions and their role in streamlining and standardizing compliance processes through the use of advanced technologies such as artificial intelligence, machine learning, and natural language processing. "Automated compliance solutions offer banks the ability to automate manual and repetitive compliance tasks, such as regulatory reporting, transaction monitoring, and risk assessments," Dr. Evans explained. "By harnessing the power of automation, banks can enhance compliance efficiency, reduce operational costs, and improve risk management practices."

Michael listened intently as Dr. Evans shared insights into

the ways in which automated compliance solutions could help banks address the challenges of regulatory compliance more effectively. "These solutions enable banks to automate routine compliance tasks, freeing up compliance professionals to focus on more strategic and value-added activities," Dr. Evans remarked. "By leveraging automation, banks can enhance their compliance capabilities, reduce the risk of human error, and improve overall compliance outcomes."

Their discussion then turned to real-life examples of banks that had successfully implemented automated compliance solutions and reaped the benefits of enhanced compliance efficiency and effectiveness. From automated regulatory reporting to AI-powered transaction monitoring to natural language processing-based compliance risk assessments, these examples showcased the diverse ways in which automation was transforming the compliance function and driving regulatory innovation in the banking industry.

As the demonstration came to a close, Michael left the innovation lab feeling inspired by Dr. Evans' insights and the transformative potential of automated compliance solutions. He realized that by embracing automation, banks had the opportunity to revolutionize their compliance processes, enhance regulatory compliance, and unlock new opportunities for innovation and growth.

Armed with Dr. Evans' insights, Michael was eager to explore the potential of automated compliance solutions further and advocate for their adoption within his organization, knowing that they held the key to navigating the complex regulatory landscape more effectively and building a more resilient and agile banking sector.

## 9.4: Regulators' Perspectives on RegTech

In a prestigious conference hall adorned with flags of various regulatory bodies, Michael Sawyer found himself among a gathering of compliance officers and regulators assembled for a symposium on RegTech. Led by Mr. William Henderson, a distinguished regulatory official, the session promised insights into how regulators viewed the emerging field of regulatory technology.

Mr. Henderson welcomed Michael with a nod, his demeanor reflecting the authority of his position.

"Welcome, everyone," Mr. Henderson said, addressing the audience with a commanding presence. "Today, we're here to discuss the regulators' perspectives on RegTech and its implications for regulatory oversight in the banking sector."

He began by acknowledging the rapid evolution of RegTech and its potential to transform the regulatory landscape. "Regulatory technology, or RegTech, has emerged as a powerful tool for enhancing regulatory compliance and oversight," Mr. Henderson explained. "From advanced data analytics to real-time monitoring to predictive modeling, RegTech offers regulators new capabilities to monitor and enforce compliance more effectively."

Michael listened intently as Mr. Henderson shared insights into how regulators viewed the adoption of RegTech by banks and financial institutions. "Regulators recognize the potential of RegTech to improve regulatory compliance, enhance market transparency, and reduce systemic risk," Mr. Henderson remarked. "However, they also recognize the need for careful oversight to ensure that RegTech solutions are implemented in a responsible and ethical manner."

Their discussion then turned to the regulatory considerations surrounding the use of RegTech, including data privacy and security, algorithmic transparency, and regulatory sandboxes. "Regulators play a critical role in fostering innovation while safeguarding the integrity and stability of the financial system," Mr. Henderson emphasized. "By engaging with industry stakeholders and promoting collaboration, regulators can help facilitate the responsible adoption of RegTech and ensure that its benefits are realized while mitigating potential risks."

As the symposium came to a close, Michael left the conference hall feeling enlightened by Mr. Henderson's insights and the regulators' perspectives on RegTech. He realized that by understanding regulators' viewpoints on RegTech, banks could navigate the regulatory landscape more effectively and build trust with regulators as they embraced innovative compliance solutions.

Armed with Mr. Henderson's insights, Michael was eager to engage with regulators and advocate for the responsible adoption of RegTech within his organization, knowing that it held the key to enhancing compliance efficiency and effectiveness while maintaining regulatory compliance and integrity.

## 9.5: Adoption Strategies for RegTech Solutions

In a bustling conference hall filled with eager attendees, Michael Sawyer found himself among a group of compliance professionals gathered for a workshop on adoption strategies for RegTech solutions. Led by Ms. Sophia Patel, a renowned expert in technology implementation, the session promised to provide practical guidance on integrating RegTech into banks' compliance processes.

Ms. Patel welcomed Michael with a warm smile, her enthusiasm for technology adoption evident in her vibrant demeanor.

"Good morning, everyone," Ms. Patel greeted the audience with a cheerful tone. "Today, we're here to explore adoption strategies for RegTech solutions and how banks can successfully integrate these innovative technologies into their compliance frameworks."

She began by emphasizing the importance of a strategic approach to RegTech adoption, highlighting the need for clear goals, stakeholder buy-in, and effective change management. "RegTech adoption is not just about implementing new technologies; it's about transforming compliance processes and driving organizational change," Ms. Patel explained. "By adopting a structured approach, banks can maximize the value of RegTech solutions and ensure successful implementation."

Michael listened intently as Ms. Patel shared insights into the key components of a successful RegTech adoption strategy, including assessing compliance needs, evaluating available solutions, and selecting the right technology partners. "Banks must first identify their compliance pain points and prioritize areas where RegTech can deliver the greatest impact," Ms. Patel remarked. "They should then conduct thorough due diligence to evaluate RegTech solutions, considering factors such as functionality, scalability, and regulatory compliance."

Their discussion then turned to best practices for implementing RegTech solutions, including pilot testing, staff training, and ongoing monitoring and evaluation. "Successful RegTech adoption requires collaboration across departments and effective communication throughout the organization," Ms. Patel emphasized. "By involving compliance professionals, IT teams, and senior leadership early in the process, banks can ensure alignment with business objectives and facilitate a smooth transition to RegTech-enabled compliance processes."

As the workshop came to a close, Michael left the conference hall feeling empowered by Ms. Patel's insights and the practical strategies for RegTech adoption. He realized that by embracing innovation and adopting a strategic approach to RegTech implementation, banks could enhance their compliance capabilities, reduce operational costs, and improve risk management practices.

Armed with Ms. Patel's guidance, Michael was ready to champion RegTech adoption within his organization, knowing that it held the key to navigating the regulatory landscape more effectively and building a more resilient and agile compliance framework.

## 9.6: Future Trends in Compliance and Regulation

In a futuristic seminar hall adorned with holographic displays, Michael Sawyer found himself among a group of forward-thinking compliance professionals gathered for a symposium on future trends in compliance and regulation. Led by Dr. Elizabeth Wang, a visionary strategist in regulatory affairs, the session promised to unveil insights into the evolving regulatory landscape and its implications for the banking industry.

Dr. Wang welcomed Michael with a nod, her aura exuding an air of anticipation for the transformative discussions ahead.

"Welcome, everyone," Dr. Wang began, her voice projecting with clarity across the hall. "Today, we're here to explore the future trends shaping compliance and regulation in the banking sector and how banks can prepare for the challenges and opportunities ahead."

She began by delving into the emerging trends reshaping the regulatory landscape, from the growing focus on data privacy and cybersecurity to the rise of RegTech and supervisory technology (SupTech) solutions. "The regulatory landscape is evolving at an unprecedented pace, driven by advancements in technology, changing consumer expectations, and shifting geopolitical dynamics," Dr. Wang explained. "Banks must anticipate and adapt to these trends to remain compliant and competitive in an increasingly complex and interconnected global economy."

Michael listened intently as Dr. Wang shared insights into the future direction of regulatory oversight, including the adoption of innovative technologies such as artificial intelligence, blockchain, and cloud computing to enhance regulatory compliance and supervisory processes. "Regulators are increasingly leveraging technology to enhance their oversight capabilities, from conducting real-time monitoring to analyzing big data to identifying emerging risks," Dr. Wang remarked. "Banks must embrace these technologies and collaborate with regulators to foster innovation and ensure regulatory compliance."

Their discussion then turned to the implications of future trends in compliance and regulation for banks, including the need for agility, resilience, and continuous learning. "The regulatory landscape is dynamic and constantly evolving, requiring banks to adopt a proactive and adaptive approach to compliance," Dr. Wang emphasized. "By staying abreast of emerging trends, investing in technology, and fostering a culture of compliance, banks can navigate the regulatory landscape more effectively and capitalize on new opportunities for innovation and growth."

As the symposium came to a close, Michael left the seminar hall feeling inspired by Dr. Wang's insights and the collective vision for the future of compliance and regulation. He realized that by embracing innovation, anticipating future trends, and collaborating with regulators, banks could navigate the regulatory landscape more effectively and build a more resilient and agile compliance framework.

Armed with Dr. Wang's foresight, Michael was ready to embark on the journey towards a future of compliance excellence, knowing that it held the key to unlocking new opportunities and driving sustainable growth in the banking industry.

# 10

# Chapter 10: The Future of Money: Cryptocurrencies and Central Bank Digital Currencies (CBDCs)

## 10.1: Understanding Cryptocurrencies

In a sleek conference room illuminated by the glow of digital screens, Michael Sawyer found himself among a diverse group of finance professionals gathered for a seminar on cryptocurrencies. Led by Professor Emily Chen, a renowned expert in blockchain technology, the session promised to demystify the enigmatic world of digital currencies.

Professor Chen welcomed Michael with a warm smile, her passion for the subject evident in her vibrant demeanor.

"Welcome, everyone," Professor Chen greeted the audience with enthusiasm. "Today, we're here to explore the fascinating world of cryptocurrencies and their potential to reshape the future of money."

She began by explaining the fundamentals of cryptocurrencies, from the revolutionary concept of blockchain technology to the decentralized nature of digital currencies. "Cryptocurrencies are digital assets that utilize cryptographic techniques to secure transactions and control the creation of new units," Professor Chen explained. "They operate on decentralized networks, such as blockchain, which enable peer-to-peer transactions without the need for intermediaries like banks or governments."

Michael listened intently as Professor Chen delved into the origins of cryptocurrencies, tracing their roots back to the invention of Bitcoin by the mysterious Satoshi Nakamoto in 2008. "Bitcoin, the first cryptocurrency, introduced the world to the concept of digital scarcity and decentralized finance," Professor Chen remarked. "Since then, thousands of cryptocurrencies have emerged, each with its unique features, use cases, and underlying technologies."

Their discussion then turned to the key characteristics of cryptocurrencies, including transparency, immutability, and censorship resistance. "Cryptocurrencies offer numerous advantages over traditional fiat currencies, such as lower transaction costs, faster settlement times, and greater financial inclusivity," Professor Chen emphasized. "However, they also pose challenges, including regulatory uncertainty, volatility, and security risks."

As the seminar came to a close, Michael left the conference room feeling enlightened by Professor Chen's insights and the intricate world of cryptocurrencies. He realized that by understanding the fundamentals of digital currencies, banks could adapt to the changing landscape of finance and capitalize on the opportunities presented by this emerging asset class.

Armed with Professor Chen's knowledge, Michael was eager to explore the potential of cryptocurrencies further and advocate for their responsible integration within his organization, knowing that they held the key to unlocking new possibilities and driving innovation in the future of money.

## 10.2: Bitcoin and Beyond: Altcoins and Tokens

In a vibrant auditorium pulsating with energy, Michael Sawyer found himself amidst a crowd of eager cryptocurrency enthusiasts gathered for a seminar on altcoins and tokens. Led by Dr. Sophia Nguyen, a trailblazing researcher in digital assets, the session promised to unveil the vast landscape beyond Bitcoin.

Dr. Nguyen welcomed Michael with a nod, her presence commanding attention as she stood before the eager audience.

"Welcome, everyone," Dr. Nguyen began, her voice echoing with excitement. "Today, we embark on a journey into the expansive world of altcoins and tokens, where innovation knows no bounds."

She started by elucidating the concept of altcoins, cryptocurrencies other than Bitcoin, and tokens, digital assets issued on existing blockchain platforms. "While Bitcoin paved the way for cryptocurrencies, altcoins and tokens have diversified the landscape, offering unique features and use cases," Dr. Nguyen explained. "From Ethereum's smart contract capabilities to Ripple's cross-border payment solutions, each altcoin and token brings its own set of innovations to the table."

Michael listened intently as Dr. Nguyen delved into the diverse array of altcoins and tokens, from the privacy-focused Monero to the stablecoin Tether. "Altcoins and tokens cater to a wide range of needs and preferences, whether it's privacy, scalability, or stability," Dr. Nguyen remarked. "They enable experimentation and innovation in the digital asset space, driving forward the evolution of decentralized finance."

Their discussion then turned to the rapid proliferation of new altcoins and tokens, fueled by crowdfunding mechanisms such as initial coin offerings (ICOs) and decentralized finance (DeFi) protocols. "The democratization of fundraising through ICOs and the expansion of DeFi have empowered entrepreneurs and developers to bring their ideas to life," Dr. Nguyen emphasized. "However, they also pose risks, including regulatory scrutiny, market volatility, and security vulnerabilities."

As the seminar reached its conclusion, Michael left the auditorium feeling inspired by Dr. Nguyen's insights and the boundless possibilities of altcoins and tokens. He realized that by embracing the diversity of digital assets and staying informed about emerging trends, banks could position themselves at the forefront of innovation in the future of money.

Armed with Dr. Nguyen's knowledge, Michael was eager to explore the potential of altcoins and tokens further and advocate for their responsible integration within his organization, knowing that they held the key to unlocking new opportunities and driving innovation in the digital economy.

## 10.3: Challenges and Opportunities of Cryptocurrency Adoption

In a bustling seminar hall, Michael Sawyer found himself among a diverse group of financial professionals gathered to discuss the challenges and opportunities of cryptocurrency adoption. Led by Dr. Emma Garcia, a seasoned expert in digital finance, the session promised to shed light on the complexities of integrating cryptocurrencies into the mainstream financial landscape.

Dr. Garcia welcomed Michael with a warm smile, her aura exuding a blend of confidence and curiosity.

"Welcome, everyone," Dr. Garcia began, her voice resonating with authority. "Today, we're here to explore the challenges and opportunities that accompany the adoption of cryptocurrencies as a medium of exchange, investment, and store of value."

She started by acknowledging the transformative potential of cryptocurrencies, from enabling borderless transactions to fostering financial inclusivity. "Cryptocurrencies hold the promise of revolutionizing the way we transact, invest, and store wealth," Dr. Garcia explained. "However, their adoption also presents a myriad of challenges, ranging from regulatory uncertainty to technological limitations."

Michael listened intently as Dr. Garcia delved into the key challenges facing cryptocurrency adoption, including regulatory scrutiny, market volatility, and security risks. "Regulatory uncertainty remains a significant barrier to widespread cryptocurrency adoption, with governments grappling to establish clear frameworks for oversight," Dr. Garcia remarked. "Moreover, the inherent volatility of cryptocurrencies poses challenges for investors and merchants alike, complicating price stability and risk management."

Their discussion then turned to the opportunities afforded by cryptocurrency adoption, including financial innovation, enhanced privacy, and access to decentralized finance (DeFi) solutions. "Cryptocurrencies have the potential to democratize access to financial services, particularly in underserved regions where traditional banking infrastructure is lacking," Dr. Garcia emphasized. "Furthermore, the emergence of DeFi platforms offers new avenues for lending, borrowing, and asset management, empowering individuals to take control of their finances."

As the seminar drew to a close, Michael left the hall feeling invigorated by Dr. Garcia's insights and the dynamic discourse on cryptocurrency adoption. He realized that while challenges abound, the opportunities presented by cryptocurrencies were too significant to ignore.

Armed with Dr. Garcia's knowledge, Michael was determined to navigate the complexities of cryptocurrency adoption within his organization, knowing that with careful consideration and strategic planning, they could unlock the transformative potential of digital assets and shape the future of finance.

## 10.4: Central Bank Digital Currencies (CBDCs): Concept and Implementation

In a prestigious conference hall adorned with the flags of nations, Michael Sawyer found himself among a gathering of esteemed economists, policymakers, and central bank representatives convened to discuss the concept and implementation of Central Bank Digital Currencies (CBDCs). Led by Dr. Alexander Schmidt, a distinguished authority in monetary economics, the session promised to illuminate the transformative potential of CBDCs.

Dr. Schmidt welcomed Michael with a nod of acknowledgment, his demeanor exuding gravitas as he prepared to address the attentive audience.

"Ladies and gentlemen," Dr. Schmidt began, his voice commanding the room's attention. "Today, we stand on the precipice of a new era in monetary policy and financial innovation, as we explore the concept and implementation of Central Bank Digital Currencies, or CBDCs."

He commenced by elucidating the fundamental concept of CBDCs, digital representations of sovereign currencies issued and regulated by central banks. "CBDCs represent a paradigm shift in the way we conceive and transact with money, offering the potential for greater efficiency, financial inclusion, and policy effectiveness," Dr. Schmidt explained. "They enable central banks to issue digital currencies that are legal tender, backed by the full faith and credit of the issuing authority."

Michael listened intently as Dr. Schmidt delved into the diverse models and approaches to CBDC implementation, from retail CBDCs accessible to the general public to wholesale CBDCs designed for interbank settlements. "The design and implementation of CBDCs require careful consideration of various factors, including privacy, security, and monetary policy objectives," Dr. Schmidt remarked. "Central banks must navigate a complex landscape of technological, regulatory, and operational challenges to ensure the successful launch and operation of CBDCs."

Their discussion then turned to the potential benefits of CBDCs, including enhanced financial inclusion, reduced transaction costs, and improved monetary policy transmission mechanisms. "CBDCs have the potential to democratize access to financial services, particularly for underserved populations," Dr. Schmidt emphasized. "Moreover, they offer central banks greater visibility into monetary flows, enabling more effective policy implementation and financial stability."

As the session concluded, Michael left the conference hall feeling inspired by Dr. Schmidt's insights and the profound implications of CBDCs for the future of money. He realized that CBDCs represented a significant step towards digital sovereignty and financial empowerment, offering new opportunities for central banks to modernize their monetary systems and enhance the welfare of their citizens.

Armed with Dr. Schmidt's knowledge, Michael was eager to explore the potential of CBDCs further and advocate for their responsible implementation within his organization, knowing that they held the key to unlocking new possibilities and driving innovation in the global financial landscape.

## 10.5: The Role of CBDCs in Financial Systems

In a grand auditorium pulsating with anticipation, Michael Sawyer found himself amidst a crowd of policymakers, economists, and technologists gathered to explore the role of Central Bank Digital Currencies (CBDCs) in shaping the future of financial systems. Led by Dr. Sofia Ramirez, a visionary economist renowned for her expertise in monetary policy, the session promised to unveil the transformative potential of CBDCs.

Dr. Ramirez welcomed Michael with a nod of recognition, her presence commanding the attention of the assembled audience.

"Ladies and gentlemen," Dr. Ramirez began, her voice resonating with authority. "Today, we embark on a journey to understand the pivotal role of Central Bank Digital Currencies, or CBDCs, in revolutionizing our financial systems and ushering in a new era of digital finance."

She commenced by elucidating the profound implications of CBDCs on monetary policy, financial stability, and economic development. "CBDCs represent a paradigm shift in the way central banks conduct monetary policy and manage financial systems," Dr. Ramirez explained. "By digitizing sovereign currencies, CBDCs offer central banks unprecedented control over the money supply, payment infrastructure, and financial intermediation."

Michael listened intently as Dr. Ramirez delved into the multifaceted role of CBDCs in modernizing financial systems, from facilitating real-time payments to fostering financial inclusion. "CBDCs have the potential to democratize access to financial services, particularly in regions with limited banking infrastructure," Dr. Ramirez remarked. "They offer a secure and efficient means of transacting, saving, and investing, thereby empowering individuals and businesses to participate fully in the digital economy."

Their discussion then turned to the implications of CBDCs for monetary policy transmission mechanisms, financial stability, and cross-border payments. "CBDCs enable central banks to implement monetary policy more effectively, mitigate systemic risks, and enhance the resilience of financial systems," Dr. Ramirez emphasized. "Moreover, they offer the potential to streamline cross-border payments, reduce transaction costs, and enhance transparency in international finance."

As the session concluded, Michael left the auditorium feeling invigorated by Dr. Ramirez's insights and the profound impact of CBDCs on the future of financial systems. He realized that CBDCs represented a transformative tool for central banks to modernize their monetary systems, foster financial inclusion, and promote economic prosperity.

Armed with Dr. Ramirez's knowledge, Michael was eager to explore the potential of CBDCs further and advocate for their responsible implementation within his organization, knowing that they held the key to unlocking new possibilities and driving innovation in the global financial landscape.

## 10.6: Implications for Traditional Banking and Monetary Policy

In a prestigious banking conference hall, Michael Sawyer found himself among a gathering of bankers, economists, and policymakers convened to explore the implications of Central Bank Digital Currencies (CBDCs) for traditional banking and monetary policy. Led by Dr. Evelyn Park, a distinguished economist with a wealth of experience in financial regulation, the session promised to unveil the transformative potential of CBDCs on the banking landscape.

Dr. Park welcomed Michael with a nod of acknowledgment, her presence exuding a sense of authority and expertise.

"Esteemed colleagues," Dr. Park began, her voice resonating with clarity. "Today, we delve into the implications of Central Bank Digital Currencies, or CBDCs, for traditional banking institutions and monetary policy frameworks."

She commenced by elucidating the profound impact of CBDCs on the banking sector, from payment systems to financial intermediation. "CBDCs have the potential to disrupt traditional banking models by providing a direct means of accessing central bank money," Dr. Park explained. "This could reshape the role of banks as intermediaries in the payments ecosystem and pose challenges to their business models."

Michael listened intently as Dr. Park delved into the implications of CBDCs for monetary policy transmission mechanisms, interest rate management, and financial stability. "CBDCs offer central banks greater control over the money supply and payment infrastructure, enabling more precise implementation of monetary policy," Dr. Park remarked. "However, they also raise questions about the transmission channels of monetary policy and the effectiveness of traditional policy tools in a digital economy."

Their discussion then turned to the potential risks and opportunities for traditional banks in the era of CBDCs. "While CBDCs present challenges for traditional banks, such as disintermediation and competition from digital currencies, they also offer opportunities for innovation and collaboration," Dr. Park emphasized. "Banks can leverage CBDCs to enhance their service offerings, streamline operations, and expand their customer base."

As the session concluded, Michael left the conference hall feeling enlightened by Dr. Park's insights and the dynamic discourse on the implications of CBDCs for traditional banking and monetary policy. He realized that while CBDCs posed challenges for traditional banks, they also opened new avenues for innovation and partnership in the evolving digital economy.

Armed with Dr. Park's knowledge, Michael was determined to navigate the complexities of CBDCs within his organization, knowing that they held the key to unlocking new opportunities and driving innovation in the global financial landscape.

# 11

# Chapter 11: Biometric Authentication and Security

## 11.1: The Need for Stronger Authentication Methods

In a state-of-the-art cybersecurity conference hall, Michael Sawyer found himself among a gathering of cybersecurity experts, technologists, and policymakers convened to address the pressing need for stronger authentication methods in the digital realm. Led by Dr. Emily Chen, a renowned cybersecurity researcher known for her expertise in biometric authentication, the session promised to shed light on the critical importance of enhancing authentication measures to combat cyber threats.

Dr. Chen welcomed Michael with a nod of acknowledgment, her presence commanding the attention of the assembled audience.

"Ladies and gentlemen," Dr. Chen began, her voice resonating with urgency. "Today, we confront the imperative need for stronger authentication methods in the face of escalating cyber threats and data breaches."

She commenced by elucidating the vulnerabilities of traditional authentication methods, such as passwords and PINs, in the digital age. "Traditional authentication methods are no longer sufficient to protect sensitive data and secure critical systems," Dr. Chen explained. "They are prone to vulnerabilities, such as password theft, phishing attacks, and social engineering, posing significant risks to individuals and organizations."

Michael listened intently as Dr. Chen delved into the transformative potential of biometric authentication in addressing the shortcomings of traditional methods. "Biometric authentication offers a more secure and convenient means of verifying identity, leveraging unique biological traits, such as fingerprints, iris patterns, and facial features," Dr. Chen remarked. "By integrating biometric factors into authentication processes, we can enhance security, reduce fraud, and improve user experience."

Their discussion then turned to the ethical and privacy considerations surrounding biometric authentication, including data protection, consent, and algorithm bias. "While biometric authentication offers significant benefits, it also raises concerns about privacy, consent, and algorithmic fairness," Dr. Chen emphasized. "It is essential to implement robust privacy safeguards and ethical guidelines to ensure the responsible use of biometric data."

As the session concluded, Michael left the conference hall feeling enlightened by Dr. Chen's insights and the dynamic discourse on the need for stronger authentication methods. He realized that while traditional authentication methods were susceptible to exploitation, biometric authentication offered a promising solution to safeguarding digital assets and protecting sensitive information.

Armed with Dr. Chen's knowledge, Michael was determined to advocate for the adoption of biometric authentication within his organization, knowing that it held the key to enhancing security and mitigating cyber risks in an increasingly interconnected world.

## 11.2: Biometric Technologies in Banking

In a sleek, modern banking conference room, Michael Sawyer found himself amidst a gathering of banking executives, security specialists, and technology experts convened to explore the integration of biometric technologies in the banking sector. Led by Dr. Sophia Reynolds, a distinguished biometric researcher known for her pioneering work in identity verification, the session promised to illuminate the transformative potential of biometrics in bolstering security and enhancing user experience in banking.

Dr. Reynolds welcomed Michael with a nod of recognition, her presence exuding a sense of authority and expertise.

"Esteemed colleagues," Dr. Reynolds began, her voice carrying a note of excitement. "Today, we delve into the realm of biometric technologies and their pivotal role in revolutionizing banking security and authentication."

She commenced by elucidating the limitations of traditional authentication methods in banking, highlighting the vulnerabilities of passwords and PINs to fraud and identity theft. "Traditional authentication methods are no longer sufficient to combat the sophisticated cyber threats facing the banking sector," Dr. Reynolds explained. "Biometric technologies offer a paradigm shift in authentication, leveraging unique biological traits to verify identity with a high degree of accuracy and reliability."

Michael listened intently as Dr. Reynolds delved into the diverse applications of biometric technologies in banking, from fingerprint recognition to facial and voice authentication. "Biometric technologies enable banks to authenticate customers seamlessly and securely across various channels, including mobile banking apps, ATMs, and branch visits," Dr. Reynolds remarked. "They enhance security, streamline authentication processes, and improve the overall user experience, fostering trust and confidence among customers."

Their discussion then turned to the regulatory and ethical considerations surrounding the use of biometric technologies in banking, including data privacy, consent, and transparency. "While biometric technologies offer significant benefits, they also raise important questions about privacy, data protection, and ethical use," Dr. Reynolds emphasized. "It is imperative for banks to implement robust security measures and adhere to stringent regulatory standards to safeguard customer data and ensure responsible use of biometric technology."

As the session concluded, Michael left the conference room feeling inspired by Dr. Reynolds's insights and the transformative potential of biometric technologies in banking. He realized that biometric authentication offered a powerful solution to strengthen security and enhance customer experience, positioning banks at the forefront of innovation in the digital age.

Armed with Dr. Reynolds's knowledge, Michael was determined to champion the adoption of biometric technologies within his organization, knowing that they held the key to safeguarding customer identities and building trust in an increasingly digital banking landscape.

## 11.3: Advantages and Limitations of Biometric Authentication

In a bustling technology laboratory, Michael Sawyer found himself surrounded by a group of researchers, cybersecurity experts, and industry professionals gathered to explore the advantages and limitations of biometric authentication. Led by Dr. Benjamin Hayes, a leading authority in biometric security, the session promised to shed light on the intricate balance between the benefits and challenges of biometric authentication.

Dr. Hayes welcomed Michael with a warm smile, his demeanor exuding a sense of intellectual curiosity and analytical rigor.

"Good morning, everyone," Dr. Hayes greeted, his voice resonating with enthusiasm. "Today, we embark on a journey to dissect the advantages and limitations of biometric authentication, a cornerstone of modern security protocols."

He commenced by elucidating the advantages of biometric authentication, highlighting its unparalleled accuracy, reliability, and convenience compared to traditional authentication methods. "Biometric authentication offers a unique blend of security and usability, leveraging intrinsic biological traits to verify identity with a high degree of certainty," Dr. Hayes explained. "It eliminates the need for complex passwords and PINs, streamlines authentication processes, and enhances the overall user experience."

Michael listened intently as Dr. Hayes delved into the

diverse applications of biometric authentication across various industries, from banking and healthcare to government and law enforcement. "Biometric authentication holds promise in a wide range of applications, including access control, identity verification, and fraud prevention," Dr. Hayes remarked. "It enables organizations to strengthen security, mitigate risks, and protect sensitive data from unauthorized access."

Their discussion then turned to the limitations of biometric authentication, including concerns about privacy, accuracy, and susceptibility to spoofing attacks. "While biometric authentication offers significant advantages, it also poses challenges, such as privacy concerns, algorithmic bias, and the potential for false positives and false negatives," Dr. Hayes emphasized. "It is essential for organizations to address these limitations through robust security measures, ethical guidelines, and ongoing research and development."

As the session concluded, Michael left the laboratory feeling enlightened by Dr. Hayes's insights and the dynamic discourse on the advantages and limitations of biometric authentication. He realized that while biometric authentication offered a powerful solution to enhance security and user experience, it also required careful consideration of its ethical and technical implications.

Armed with Dr. Hayes's knowledge, Michael was determined to navigate the complexities of biometric authentication within his organization, knowing that it held the key to unlocking new possibilities and driving innovation in the ever-evolving landscape of cybersecurity.

## 11.4: Addressing Privacy Concerns

In a dimly lit boardroom, Michael Sawyer found himself among a group of privacy advocates, legal experts, and technology professionals convened to address the pressing privacy concerns surrounding biometric authentication. Led by Dr. Sarah Johnson, a prominent privacy researcher known for her advocacy work in digital rights, the session promised to delve into the ethical and regulatory considerations of biometric data usage.

Dr. Johnson greeted Michael with a reassuring smile, her presence emanating a sense of empathy and determination.

"Good afternoon, everyone," Dr. Johnson began, her voice imbued with sincerity. "Today, we confront the critical issue of privacy in biometric authentication and explore strategies to safeguard individual rights in an increasingly digitized world."

She commenced by elucidating the privacy risks associated with biometric data usage, highlighting concerns about unauthorized access, data breaches, and potential misuse of sensitive information. "Biometric authentication poses unique privacy challenges, as it involves the collection and storage of individuals' biological traits, such as fingerprints, iris scans, and facial features," Dr. Johnson explained. "It is imperative for organizations to implement robust privacy safeguards and adhere to stringent regulatory standards to protect biometric data from exploitation and abuse."

Michael listened intently as Dr. Johnson delved into the ethical considerations surrounding the collection, storage, and usage of biometric data, emphasizing the importance of transparency, informed consent, and data minimization. "Privacy is a fundamental human right that must be respected and upheld in the design and deployment of biometric authentication systems," Dr. Johnson remarked. "Organizations must prioritize privacy by design principles, conduct privacy impact assessments, and provide individuals with clear information about how their biometric data is collected, processed, and stored."

Their discussion then turned to the regulatory landscape surrounding biometric data protection, including the General Data Protection Regulation (GDPR), the California Consumer Privacy Act (CCPA), and emerging privacy laws and regulations worldwide. "Regulatory compliance is essential to ensuring the responsible use of biometric data and maintaining trust with individuals," Dr. Johnson emphasized. "Organizations must navigate complex legal frameworks, uphold privacy rights, and demonstrate accountability in their handling of biometric information."

As the session concluded, Michael left the boardroom feeling empowered by Dr. Johnson's insights and the robust discourse on addressing privacy concerns in biometric authentication. He realized that while biometric authentication offered significant benefits in security and user experience, it also required a steadfast commitment to privacy protection and ethical governance.

Armed with Dr. Johnson's knowledge, Michael was determined to advocate for privacy-centric practices within his organization, knowing that they were essential to building trust with customers and safeguarding their fundamental rights in an increasingly digital world.

## 11.5: Biometric Security in Mobile Banking

In a bustling innovation hub, Michael Sawyer found himself amidst a gathering of mobile banking experts, cybersecurity specialists, and technology enthusiasts convened to explore the transformative role of biometric authentication in securing mobile banking applications. Led by Dr. Rebecca Chen, a distinguished mobile security researcher known for her groundbreaking work in biometric authentication, the session promised to unveil the future of secure and seamless banking on the go.

Dr. Chen greeted Michael with a warm smile, her demeanor radiating confidence and expertise.

"Good morning, everyone," Dr. Chen began, her voice resonating with passion. "Today, we embark on a journey to revolutionize mobile banking security through the power of biometric authentication."

She commenced by elucidating the inherent vulnerabilities of traditional authentication methods in mobile banking, highlighting the risks of password theft, phishing attacks, and device compromise. "Mobile banking applications are prime targets for cybercriminals due to the sensitive financial information they contain," Dr. Chen explained. "Biometric authentication offers a robust solution to mitigate these risks, providing secure and frictionless access to mobile banking services."

Michael listened intently as Dr. Chen delved into the advantages of biometric security in mobile banking, emphasizing its seamless integration with existing mobile devices and its ability to enhance user experience while ensuring strong authentication. "Biometric authentication allows users to access their mobile banking accounts with a simple touch of their finger or a glance of their face, eliminating the need for cumbersome passwords and PINs," Dr. Chen remarked. "It provides a seamless and intuitive user experience, increasing convenience and driving adoption of mobile banking services."

Their discussion then turned to the technical considerations of implementing biometric authentication in mobile banking applications, including device compatibility, sensor accuracy, and algorithmic performance. "Biometric authentication requires careful implementation to ensure compatibility across various mobile devices and operating systems," Dr. Chen emphasized. "It also necessitates robust security measures to protect biometric data from unauthorized access and tampering."

As the session concluded, Michael left the innovation hub feeling inspired by Dr. Chen's insights and the dynamic discourse on biometric security in mobile banking. He realized that biometric authentication offered a transformative solution to enhance security, streamline user experience, and drive innovation in the mobile banking landscape.

Armed with Dr. Chen's knowledge, Michael was determined to champion the adoption of biometric security within his organization's mobile banking app, knowing that it held the key to building trust with customers and staying ahead of evolving cybersecurity threats in an increasingly mobile-driven world.

## 11.6: Future Development in Biometric Authentication

In a cutting-edge research facility, Michael Sawyer found himself among a group of forward-thinking scientists, engineers, and technology innovators convened to explore the frontiers of biometric authentication. Led by Dr. Alexander Nguyen, a visionary researcher renowned for his pioneering work in biometric technologies, the session promised to unveil the future of authentication and identity verification.

Dr. Nguyen welcomed Michael with a nod of recognition, his eyes sparkling with excitement and anticipation.

"Welcome, everyone," Dr. Nguyen began, his voice echoing with enthusiasm. "Today, we embark on a journey to push the boundaries of biometric authentication and unlock new possibilities for security and identity verification."

He commenced by elucidating the latest advancements in biometric technologies, from multimodal authentication to behavioral biometrics and beyond. "The future of biometric authentication lies in its ability to harness the richness and diversity of human characteristics," Dr. Nguyen explained. "By combining multiple biometric modalities, such as fingerprints, facial features, and voice patterns, we can create more robust and resilient authentication systems."

Michael listened intently as Dr. Nguyen delved into the potential applications of behavioral biometrics, such as gait analysis, keystroke dynamics, and even brainwave patterns, in enhancing security and user experience. "Behavioral biometrics offer a dynamic and continuous authentication approach, allowing organizations to verify users based on their unique behavioral traits," Dr. Nguyen remarked. "This not only strengthens security but also enables frictionless authentication across various touchpoints, from mobile devices to IoT devices."

Their discussion then turned to the future challenges and opportunities in biometric authentication, including concerns about algorithmic bias, ethical implications, and the need for interoperability and standardization. "As we venture into uncharted territories, it is essential for researchers, industry stakeholders, and policymakers to collaborate closely to address emerging challenges and pave the way for responsible innovation," Dr. Nguyen emphasized. "Together, we can shape a future where biometric authentication is not only secure and reliable but also inclusive and ethical."

As the session concluded, Michael left the research facility feeling inspired by Dr. Nguyen's insights and the vision for future developments in biometric authentication. He realized that while the journey ahead was fraught with challenges and uncertainties, it also held immense potential to redefine the way we authenticate and verify identity in an increasingly digital and interconnected world.

Armed with Dr. Nguyen's vision, Michael was determined to contribute to the advancement of biometric authentication within his organization, knowing that it was not just about securing data but also empowering individuals to navigate the digital landscape with confidence and trust.

# 12

# Chapter 12: Wealth Management in the Digital Age

## 12.1: The Changing Landscape of Wealth Management

In a sleek conference room overlooking the city skyline, Michael Sawyer found himself among a group of seasoned wealth managers, financial advisors, and technology disruptors gathered to explore the evolving landscape of wealth management in the digital age. Led by Professor Emily Collins, a renowned expert in financial innovation and digital transformation, the session promised to unveil the seismic shifts reshaping the wealth management industry.

Professor Collins greeted Michael with a warm smile, her presence exuding a sense of wisdom and authority.

"Good morning, everyone," Professor Collins began, her voice commanding attention. "Today, we embark on a journey to navigate the changing landscape of wealth management and uncover the opportunities and challenges that lie ahead."

She commenced by elucidating the traditional paradigms of

## CHAPTER 12: WEALTH MANAGEMENT IN THE DIGITAL AGE

wealth management, highlighting the role of financial advisors, brokerage firms, and investment banks in providing personalized financial advice and portfolio management services. "For decades, the wealth management industry has operated within well-defined boundaries, guided by established practices and conventional wisdom," Professor Collins explained. "However, the emergence of digital technologies and shifting consumer preferences are revolutionizing the way we manage wealth, presenting both opportunities and disruptions for industry incumbents."

Michael listened intently as Professor Collins delved into the drivers of change reshaping wealth management, including technological innovation, regulatory reforms, and demographic shifts. "The rise of digital platforms, robo-advisors, and online brokerages is democratizing access to wealth management services, empowering individuals to take control of their financial futures," Professor Collins remarked. "At the same time, regulatory changes, such as the fiduciary rule and MiFID II, are raising the bar for transparency, accountability, and client-centricity in the industry."

Their discussion then turned to the implications of digital transformation on traditional wealth management firms, including the need to adapt to changing client expectations, embrace digital tools and analytics, and differentiate through personalized advice and holistic financial planning. "In the digital age, success in wealth management hinges on the ability to leverage technology to deliver tailored solutions, engage clients on their terms, and build trust through transparency and integrity," Professor Collins emphasized. "Firms that embrace innovation and agility will thrive in this new era of wealth management, while those that resist change risk being left behind."

As the session concluded, Michael left the conference room feeling inspired by Professor Collins's insights and the dynamic discourse on the changing landscape of wealth management. He realized that while the road ahead was fraught with uncertainties and disruptions, it also held immense opportunities for those willing to embrace innovation and adapt to the evolving needs of clients in the digital age.

Armed with Professor Collins's wisdom, Michael was determined to navigate the complexities of wealth management within his organization, knowing that success lay not just in managing assets but also in empowering individuals to achieve their financial goals and aspirations in a rapidly changing world.

## 12.2: Robo-Advisors vs. Traditional Financial Advisors

In a bustling financial district, Michael Sawyer found himself amidst a heated debate between proponents of robo-advisors and staunch defenders of traditional financial advisors. Led by Dr. Benjamin Reynolds, a distinguished economist and advocate for digital innovation in wealth management, the session promised to dissect the pros and cons of robo-advisors and traditional financial advisors in navigating the complexities of investment management.

Dr. Reynolds greeted Michael with a firm handshake, his demeanor exuding confidence and intellect.

"Welcome, everyone," Dr. Reynolds began, his voice commanding the attention of the room. "Today, we engage in a critical discourse on the merits of robo-advisors and traditional financial advisors in delivering investment advice and portfolio management services."

He commenced by elucidating the value proposition of robo-advisors, highlighting their cost-effectiveness, accessibility, and algorithm-driven investment strategies. "Robo-advisors offer investors a low-cost alternative to traditional financial advisors, leveraging technology to automate investment decisions and rebalance portfolios," Dr. Reynolds explained. "They provide a streamlined and convenient investment experience, catering to tech-savvy individuals seeking simplified solutions and passive investment strategies."

Michael listened intently as Dr. Reynolds delved into the strengths of traditional financial advisors, including their expertise, personalized advice, and human touch. "Traditional financial advisors offer investors the benefit of human expertise and tailored financial planning services," Dr. Reynolds remarked. "They possess deep industry knowledge, experience, and intuition, enabling them to understand clients' unique goals, risk tolerance, and financial circumstances."

Their discussion then turned to the challenges and opportunities presented by the coexistence of robo-advisors and traditional financial advisors in the wealth management industry. "While robo-advisors excel in cost-efficiency and scalability, they may lack the personalized touch and emotional intelligence of traditional financial advisors," Dr. Reynolds emphasized. "Conversely, traditional financial advisors must embrace technology and digital tools to remain competitive in a rapidly evolving landscape."

As the debate raged on, Michael pondered the merits of each approach, recognizing the need for a balanced approach that harnesses the strengths of both robo-advisors and traditional financial advisors to meet the diverse needs of investors in the digital age.

Armed with Dr. Reynolds's insights, Michael was determined to advocate for a hybrid model within his organization, combining the efficiency of robo-advisors with the expertise of traditional financial advisors to deliver personalized and holistic wealth management solutions that empower clients to achieve their financial goals with confidence and clarity.

## 12.3: Personalized Investment Strategies

In a sleek boardroom adorned with financial charts and market data, Michael Sawyer found himself among a group of seasoned investment strategists, data analysts, and client advisors convened to explore the art and science of crafting personalized investment strategies. Led by Ms. Sophia Chen, a seasoned portfolio manager known for her expertise in data-driven investment solutions, the session promised to unveil the secrets behind designing tailored investment portfolios that align with clients' unique financial goals and risk preferences.

Ms. Chen greeted Michael with a warm smile, her aura radiating a blend of confidence and empathy.

"Good afternoon, everyone," Ms. Chen began, her voice resonating with authority. "Today, we embark on a journey to unlock the power of personalized investment strategies and empower our clients to achieve their financial aspirations."

She commenced by elucidating the principles of personalized investment strategies, emphasizing the importance of understanding clients' financial objectives, risk tolerance, time horizon, and liquidity needs. "Personalized investment strategies are not one-size-fits-all solutions," Ms. Chen explained. "They require a deep understanding of each client's unique circumstances and aspirations, enabling us to tailor investment portfolios that reflect their individual preferences and optimize risk-adjusted returns."

Michael listened intently as Ms. Chen delved into the methodologies and tools used to design personalized investment strategies, including asset allocation models, risk profiling assessments, and quantitative analysis techniques. "By leveraging advanced data analytics and machine learning algorithms, we can uncover insights that inform our investment decisions and optimize portfolio construction," Ms. Chen remarked. "This data-driven approach allows us to adapt investment strategies dynamically in response to changing market conditions and client preferences."

Their discussion then turned to the challenges and opportunities presented by personalized investment strategies, including the need for ongoing monitoring and rebalancing, managing behavioral biases, and communicating effectively with clients. "Personalized investment strategies require a proactive and holistic approach to client engagement," Ms. Chen emphasized. "By fostering open communication, trust, and transparency, we can build long-lasting relationships with our clients and help them navigate the complexities of the financial markets with confidence."

As the session concluded, Michael left the boardroom feeling inspired by Ms. Chen's insights and the dynamic discourse on personalized investment strategies. He realized that while the road to success was paved with challenges and uncertainties, it also held immense opportunities to create value for clients and drive innovation in the wealth management industry.

Armed with Ms. Chen's wisdom, Michael was determined to champion the adoption of personalized investment strategies within his organization, knowing that they held the key to unlocking the full potential of client portfolios and delivering sustainable long-term returns in an ever-changing market landscape.

## 12.4: Digital Tools for Portfolio Management

In a state-of-the-art innovation lab buzzing with technological fervor, Michael Sawyer found himself surrounded by a diverse team of software engineers, data scientists, and financial analysts gathered to explore the latest advancements in digital tools for portfolio management. Led by Dr. Elena Patel, a visionary technologist renowned for her pioneering work in fintech innovation, the session promised to unveil the cutting-edge technologies revolutionizing the way investment portfolios are managed and optimized.

Dr. Patel greeted Michael with a warm handshake, her eyes sparkling with enthusiasm and curiosity.

"Good morning, everyone," Dr. Patel began, her voice tinged with excitement. "Today, we embark on a journey to discover the transformative power of digital tools for portfolio management and how they are reshaping the wealth management landscape."

She commenced by elucidating the capabilities of digital tools, including portfolio optimization algorithms, risk analytics platforms, and performance attribution models. "Digital tools empower portfolio managers to harness the vast troves of data available in today's interconnected world and extract actionable insights that drive informed investment decisions," Dr. Patel explained. "By leveraging advanced analytics and artificial intelligence, we can optimize portfolio construction, mitigate risk, and enhance returns for our clients."

Michael listened intently as Dr. Patel delved into the practical applications of digital tools for portfolio management, including asset allocation optimization, factor-based investing, and scenario analysis. "Digital tools enable us to simulate various market scenarios and stress test portfolio strategies, allowing us to anticipate and mitigate potential risks before they materialize," Dr. Patel remarked. "They also facilitate real-time monitoring and rebalancing, ensuring that portfolios remain aligned with clients' investment objectives and risk preferences."

Their discussion then turned to the challenges and opportunities presented by digital tools for portfolio management, including data privacy concerns, regulatory compliance, and the need for ongoing innovation and adaptation. "As the wealth management industry embraces digital transformation, it is imperative that we maintain a steadfast commitment to integrity, transparency, and client-centricity," Dr. Patel emphasized. "By harnessing the power of digital tools responsibly, we can unlock new opportunities for value creation and deliver superior outcomes for our clients."

As the session concluded, Michael left the innovation lab feeling invigorated by Dr. Patel's insights and the dynamic discourse on digital tools for portfolio management. He realized that while the adoption of digital technologies posed its share of challenges, it also held immense potential to revolutionize the way investment portfolios are managed and optimized in the digital age.

Armed with Dr. Patel's wisdom, Michael was determined to champion the integration of digital tools within his organization, knowing that they held the key to unlocking new levels of efficiency, innovation, and value creation in portfolio management and wealth advisory services.

## 12.5: Challenges and Risks in Digital Wealth Management

Amidst the sleek glass and steel towers of the financial district, Michael Sawyer found himself in a high-level strategy session convened to address the challenges and risks inherent in digital wealth management. Led by Ms. Emily Chen, a seasoned risk management expert renowned for her foresight and strategic acumen, the session promised to shed light on the complexities and pitfalls of navigating the digital frontier in wealth management.

Ms. Chen greeted Michael with a nod of acknowledgement, her expression serious and contemplative.

"Good afternoon, everyone," Ms. Chen began, her voice commanding attention. "Today, we confront the realities of digital wealth management and the challenges that accompany the pursuit of innovation in our industry."

She commenced by elucidating the challenges posed by the rapid pace of technological change, including cybersecurity threats, data privacy concerns, and regulatory compliance. "Digital wealth management introduces new vulnerabilities and risks that must be carefully managed and mitigated," Ms. Chen explained. "From data breaches and cyber attacks to regulatory scrutiny and client distrust, the stakes are higher than ever in the digital age."

Michael listened intently as Ms. Chen delved into the complexities of safeguarding sensitive financial information, ensuring compliance with evolving regulatory frameworks, and maintaining trust and confidence among clients. "As custodians of our clients' wealth, we bear a solemn responsibility to protect their interests and safeguard their assets from harm," Ms. Chen remarked. "This requires a proactive and multi-faceted approach to risk management that encompasses technology, governance, and culture."

Their discussion then turned to the risks inherent in algorithmic trading, machine learning models, and automated decision-making processes. "While digital tools offer unprecedented opportunities for efficiency and innovation, they also introduce new sources of risk and complexity," Ms. Chen emphasized. "From algorithmic biases and model drift to operational failures and systemic vulnerabilities, the challenges of digital wealth management are as diverse as they are daunting."

As the session concluded, Michael left the boardroom feeling sobered by Ms. Chen's insights and the sobering reality of the challenges and risks inherent in digital wealth management. He realized that while the promise of innovation held immense potential for the future of wealth management, it also demanded a vigilant and unwavering commitment to integrity, diligence, and prudence in navigating the complexities of the digital frontier.

Armed with Ms. Chen's wisdom, Michael was determined to lead by example within his organization, championing a culture of risk awareness, resilience, and responsible innovation that prioritized the interests and well-being of clients above all else.

## 12.6: Hybrid Models: Blending Human Expertise with Technology

In the heart of the financial district, amidst the bustling energy of the trading floor, Michael Sawyer found himself at the forefront of a pivotal discussion on the integration of human expertise and technological innovation in wealth management. Led by Mr. James Reynolds, a visionary thought leader renowned for his foresight and strategic vision, the session promised to unveil the transformative potential of hybrid models that harmonized the best of human insight with the power of cutting-edge technology.

Mr. Reynolds greeted Michael with a firm handshake, his eyes shining with a blend of determination and curiosity.

"Good morning, everyone," Mr. Reynolds began, his voice resonating with authority. "Today, we embark on a journey to explore the convergence of human expertise and technological innovation in wealth management and the opportunities it presents for driving superior client outcomes."

He commenced by elucidating the principles of hybrid models, emphasizing the complementary nature of human judgment and technological efficiency. "Hybrid models empower wealth managers to leverage the unique strengths of both humans and machines, combining the intuition, empathy, and judgment of human advisors with the speed, accuracy, and scalability of technology," Mr. Reynolds explained. "By fostering collaboration and synergy between humans and machines, we can deliver personalized, holistic, and value-added advisory services that transcend the limitations of either approach alone."

Michael listened intently as Mr. Reynolds delved into the

practical applications of hybrid models, including algorithmic trading, robo-advisory platforms, and augmented decision support systems. "Hybrid models enable wealth managers to augment their capabilities and enhance the client experience by leveraging technology to automate routine tasks, streamline operations, and unlock new insights," Mr. Reynolds remarked. "By harnessing the power of artificial intelligence, machine learning, and predictive analytics, we can deliver tailored investment solutions that align with clients' unique goals, preferences, and risk profiles."

Their discussion then turned to the challenges and opportunities presented by hybrid models, including the need for ongoing training and upskilling, managing client expectations, and navigating regulatory complexities. "As the wealth management industry embraces hybrid models, it is imperative that we maintain a steadfast commitment to ethics, transparency, and client-centricity," Mr. Reynolds emphasized. "By empowering our advisors with the tools, resources, and support they need to thrive in the digital age, we can build stronger relationships with our clients and deliver sustainable long-term value."

As the session concluded, Michael left the trading floor feeling inspired by Mr. Reynolds' insights and the dynamic discourse on hybrid models in wealth management. He realized that while the integration of human expertise and technological innovation posed its share of challenges, it also held immense potential to revolutionize the way advisory services were delivered and experienced in the digital age.

Armed with Mr. Reynolds' wisdom, Michael was determined to champion the adoption of hybrid models within his organization, knowing that they held the key to unlocking new levels of efficiency, innovation, and value creation in wealth management and client advisory services.

# 13

# Chapter 13: Cybersecurity in Banking

## 13.1: The Growing Threat Landscape

In the heart of a bustling cybersecurity operations center, surrounded by a labyrinth of monitors displaying streams of data and threat alerts, Michael Sawyer found himself at the forefront of the battle against cyber threats in banking. Led by Dr. Sarah Adams, a renowned cybersecurity expert known for her unwavering dedication and strategic brilliance, the session promised to shed light on the evolving threat landscape facing the financial industry and the imperative of vigilance and resilience in the face of cyber adversaries.

Dr. Adams greeted Michael with a firm nod, her eyes reflecting the gravity of the challenge ahead.

"Good afternoon, everyone," Dr. Adams began, her voice commanding attention amidst the hum of activity in the room. "Today, we confront the stark realities of the cyber threat landscape in banking and the urgent need for heightened vigilance and preparedness."

She commenced by painting a vivid picture of the ever-evolving threat landscape, including the proliferation of sophisticated cyber adversaries, the rising tide of ransomware attacks, and the increasing sophistication of social engineering tactics.

"The cyber threat landscape is characterized by relentless innovation and adaptability on the part of adversaries, who continuously seek to exploit vulnerabilities and weaknesses in our defenses," Dr. Adams explained. "From nation-state actors and organized crime syndicates to lone wolf hackers and insider threats, the adversaries we face are diverse, determined, and increasingly sophisticated in their tactics and techniques."

Michael listened intently as Dr. Adams delved into the challenges posed by emerging technologies, including artificial intelligence, machine learning, and quantum computing, which promised to reshape the cybersecurity landscape in profound and unpredictable ways.

"As the financial industry embraces digital transformation, it becomes increasingly imperative that we anticipate and prepare for the security implications of new technologies," Dr. Adams remarked. "From the proliferation of connected devices and the Internet of Things to the advent of quantum computing and the rise of autonomous systems, the attack surface is expanding exponentially, presenting new challenges and opportunities for cyber defense."

Their discussion then turned to the imperative of collaboration and information sharing within the cybersecurity community, emphasizing the importance of collective defense and resilience in the face of cyber threats. "In the face of an ever-evolving and dynamic threat landscape, it is imperative that we work together as a unified front to defend against cyber adversaries and protect the integrity, confidentiality, and availability of critical financial systems and data," Dr. Adams emphasized. "By fostering collaboration and information sharing among industry stakeholders, government agencies, and law enforcement partners, we can enhance our collective ability to detect, deter, and respond to cyber threats effectively."

As the session concluded, Michael left the cybersecurity operations center feeling sobered by Dr. Adams' insights and the stark reality of the cyber threat landscape facing the financial industry. He realized that while the challenges posed by cyber adversaries were formidable, they also presented an opportunity to strengthen resilience, foster collaboration, and drive innovation in cybersecurity defense.

Armed with Dr. Adams' wisdom, Michael was determined to lead by example within his organization, championing a culture of cybersecurity awareness, preparedness, and vigilance that prioritized the protection of critical financial systems and data above all else.

## 13.2: Common Cyber Attacks in Banking

In the nerve center of a financial institution's cybersecurity hub, Michael Sawyer stood amidst a team of dedicated analysts, their eyes fixed on the myriad screens displaying real-time data and threat indicators. Led by Dr. Sarah Adams, a seasoned cybersecurity expert known for her analytical prowess and strategic foresight, the session delved into the common cyber attacks plaguing the banking sector and the imperative of vigilance and swift response in the face of adversity.

Dr. Adams surveyed the room with a steely gaze, her presence commanding attention amidst the buzz of activity.

"Good morning, everyone," Dr. Adams began, her voice cutting through the tension in the room. "Today, we confront the stark reality of common cyber attacks targeting the financial sector and the critical importance of readiness and resilience in our defense."

She commenced by detailing the most prevalent cyber threats facing banks, including phishing attacks, malware infections, and distributed denial-of-service (DDoS) assaults. "Cyber adversaries employ a variety of tactics to infiltrate financial institutions, compromise sensitive data, and disrupt operations," Dr. Adams explained. "From deceptive phishing emails and malicious attachments to sophisticated malware variants and ransomware payloads, the arsenal of cyber threats at their disposal is vast and ever-evolving."

Michael listened intently as Dr. Adams elucidated the modus operandi of each attack vector, highlighting their potential impact on financial institutions and their customers. "Phishing attacks, for instance, leverage social engineering tactics to trick unsuspecting users into divulging sensitive information or clicking on malicious links," Dr. Adams remarked. "Meanwhile, malware infections exploit vulnerabilities in software and systems to gain unauthorized access, exfiltrate data, or disrupt critical services."

Their discussion then turned to the insidious nature of DDoS attacks, which aim to overwhelm financial institutions' networks and infrastructure with a deluge of malicious traffic. "DDoS attacks pose a significant threat to the availability and integrity of financial services, rendering systems inaccessible to legitimate users and causing widespread disruption and chaos," Dr. Adams emphasized. "By flooding servers and networks with an overwhelming volume of requests, attackers can cripple operations, undermine customer trust, and inflict significant financial losses."

As the session concluded, Michael left the cybersecurity hub feeling galvanized by Dr. Adams' insights and the urgent imperative to fortify defenses against common cyber attacks in banking. He realized that while the threats posed by cyber adversaries were formidable, they also presented an opportunity to strengthen resilience, enhance detection capabilities, and foster collaboration across the financial industry.

Armed with Dr. Adams' wisdom, Michael was determined to lead his team with resolve and determination, ensuring that they remained vigilant and proactive in safeguarding their institution against the ever-present threat of cyber attacks.

## 13.3: Building a Robust Cybersecurity Framework

Within the fortified walls of a cybersecurity war room, Michael Sawyer stood alongside his team of dedicated analysts, their focus unwavering as they delved into the intricate process of constructing a robust cybersecurity framework under the guidance of Dr. Sarah Adams, a revered authority in the field.

Dr. Adams commanded the room with her presence, her steely gaze piercing through the haze of digital data displayed on the monitors.

"Good afternoon, everyone," Dr. Adams began, her voice resonating with authority. "Today, we embark on a mission to construct a fortress of defense against the relentless tide of cyber threats facing our institution."

She initiated the discussion by outlining the key components of a robust cybersecurity framework, emphasizing the importance of proactive threat detection, continuous monitoring, and rapid incident response. "A robust cybersecurity framework serves as the bedrock of our defense, providing the foundation upon which we build our resilience against cyber adversaries," Dr. Adams explained. "By implementing a multi-layered defense strategy that encompasses prevention, detection, and response capabilities, we can fortify our organization's digital perimeter and safeguard our critical assets from exploitation."

Michael listened intently as Dr. Adams elucidated the necessity of a comprehensive risk management approach, which involved identifying vulnerabilities, assessing potential threats, and prioritizing mitigation efforts. "Risk management lies at the heart of our cybersecurity framework, enabling us to assess and mitigate potential threats to our organization's security and stability," Dr. Adams remarked. "By conducting regular risk assessments, we can identify and address vulnerabilities in our systems and processes, ensuring that we remain one step ahead of cyber adversaries at all times."

Their discussion then turned to the critical importance of employee training and awareness programs in fostering a culture of cybersecurity within the organization. "Our people are our first line of defense against cyber threats, and it is imperative that we equip them with the knowledge, skills, and awareness necessary to identify and respond to potential security incidents," Dr. Adams emphasized. "By investing in comprehensive training and awareness programs, we can empower our employees to become vigilant guardians of our organization's digital assets and ambassadors of cyber resilience."

As the session concluded, Michael left the war room feeling inspired by Dr. Adams' insights and the collective determination of his team to construct a robust cybersecurity framework that would withstand the test of time. He realized that while the challenges posed by cyber threats were formidable, they also presented an opportunity to strengthen defenses, enhance capabilities, and foster a culture of cyber resilience within their organization.

Armed with Dr. Adams' wisdom, Michael was determined to lead his team with confidence and resolve, ensuring that they remained steadfast in their commitment to protecting their institution against the ever-evolving threat landscape of cyberspace.

## 13.4: Incident Response and Crisis Management

Amidst the dimly lit confines of the incident response command center, Michael Sawyer stood at the helm of his team, their eyes fixed on the array of monitors displaying a flurry of alerts and indicators. Guided by the steady hand of Dr. Sarah Adams, a seasoned veteran in the realm of incident response and crisis management, they braced themselves for the challenges that lay ahead.

Dr. Adams surveyed the room with a calm demeanor, her voice carrying a sense of reassurance amidst the palpable tension.

"Good evening, everyone," Dr. Adams began, her tone measured yet resolute. "Today, we confront the stark reality of incident response and crisis management in the face of cyber adversity."

She wasted no time in outlining the critical components of an effective incident response plan, emphasizing the importance of rapid detection, containment, and mitigation of security incidents. "In the event of a security breach or cyber attack, every second counts," Dr. Adams remarked. "Our ability to respond swiftly and decisively can mean the difference between containment and catastrophe."

Michael listened intently as Dr. Adams detailed the roles and responsibilities of each team member within the incident response framework, stressing the importance of clear communication, collaboration, and coordination under pressure. "Effective incident response requires a well-coordinated effort from all stakeholders, including IT teams, security analysts, legal counsel, and senior leadership," Dr. Adams explained. "By establishing clear lines of communication and predefined response protocols, we can ensure that everyone knows their role and responsibilities in the event of a security incident."

Their discussion then turned to the critical importance of crisis management in mitigating the reputational and financial fallout of a cyber attack. "In the aftermath of a security breach, swift and decisive action is paramount to restoring trust and confidence in our organization," Dr. Adams emphasized. "By implementing a comprehensive crisis management plan that encompasses communication strategies, stakeholder engagement, and regulatory compliance, we can minimize the impact of the incident on our customers, partners, and shareholders."

As the session concluded, Michael felt a renewed sense of confidence in their ability to navigate the storm of cyber adversity. Armed with Dr. Adams' insights and guidance, he knew that his team was well-prepared to respond effectively to any security incident or crisis that may arise.

With their incident response plan firmly in place and their crisis management strategies honed to perfection, they stood ready to confront the challenges of cyberspace with unwavering resolve and determination.

## 13.5: Cybersecurity Awareness and Training

In a state-of-the-art training facility, Michael Sawyer stood before a group of eager employees, their attention captivated by the presentation unfolding before them. Led by Dr. Sarah Adams, a renowned cybersecurity expert, the session focused on the critical importance of cybersecurity awareness and training in defending against the ever-present threat of cyber attacks.

Dr. Adams commanded the room with her expertise, her words resonating with authority as she addressed the audience.

"Good morning, everyone," Dr. Adams began, her voice carrying a sense of urgency. "Today, we embark on a journey to equip ourselves with the knowledge, skills, and awareness necessary to defend against the pervasive threat of cyber attacks."

She commenced by elucidating the various types of cyber threats facing organizations today, from phishing scams and malware infections to social engineering tactics and insider threats. "Cyber adversaries are constantly evolving their tactics and techniques to infiltrate our networks, compromise our data, and disrupt our operations," Dr. Adams explained. "It is imperative that we remain vigilant and proactive in our defense against these threats."

Michael listened intently as Dr. Adams outlined the key principles of cybersecurity awareness, emphasizing the importance of recognizing and reporting suspicious activity, adhering to security policies and procedures, and maintaining good cyber hygiene practices. "Our people are our greatest asset in the fight against cybercrime," Dr. Adams remarked. "By empowering them with the knowledge and skills to identify and mitigate potential threats, we can create a culture of cybersecurity awareness that permeates throughout our organization."

Their discussion then turned to the critical role of cybersecurity training in arming employees with the tools and techniques necessary to defend against cyber attacks. "Cybersecurity training is not a one-time event, but an ongoing process of learning and development," Dr. Adams emphasized. "Through interactive workshops, simulated phishing exercises, and real-world scenarios, we can provide our employees with the hands-on experience and practical skills needed to navigate the complex landscape of cyberspace."

As the session concluded, Michael felt a renewed sense of purpose and determination. Armed with Dr. Adams' insights and guidance, he knew that their organization was well-equipped to defend against the ever-evolving threat of cyber attacks.

With cybersecurity awareness ingrained in their culture and training programs tailored to their specific needs, they stood ready to confront the challenges of cyberspace with confidence and resilience.

## 13.6: Collaborative Approaches to Cyber Defense

In a high-level meeting room adorned with state-of-the-art technology, Michael Sawyer convened with a consortium of industry leaders, government officials, and cybersecurity experts. Led by Dr. Sarah Adams, a trailblazer in the field of collaborative cyber defense, the gathering aimed to forge alliances and partnerships in the ongoing battle against cyber threats.

Dr. Adams commanded the room with her unwavering presence, her voice resonating with authority as she addressed the assembly.

"Good afternoon, esteemed colleagues," Dr. Adams began, her tone brimming with conviction. "Today, we stand united in our shared mission to defend against the relentless onslaught of cyber adversaries."

She commenced by elucidating the principles of collaborative cyber defense, emphasizing the importance of information sharing, threat intelligence sharing, and joint incident response efforts. "Cyber threats know no boundaries, and neither should our defenses," Dr. Adams remarked. "By fostering collaboration and cooperation among industry stakeholders, government agencies, and cybersecurity professionals, we can create a united front against cybercrime."

Michael listened intently as Dr. Adams outlined the various collaborative initiatives and partnerships that were instrumental in enhancing cyber defense capabilities across sectors. From information sharing platforms and threat intelligence networks to joint training exercises and coordinated response efforts, these initiatives exemplified the power of collaboration in the fight against cyber threats.

Their discussion then turned to the critical role of public-private partnerships in bolstering cyber resilience and safeguarding critical infrastructure. "Cybersecurity is a collective responsibility that requires the collective effort of all stakeholders," Dr. Adams emphasized. "By forging strong partnerships between government, industry, and academia, we can leverage our collective expertise, resources, and capabilities to address the evolving threat landscape of cyberspace."

As the meeting concluded, Michael felt a renewed sense of optimism and resolve. Armed with Dr. Adams' insights and the collective determination of his peers, he knew that their collaborative efforts would strengthen their defenses and elevate their cyber resilience to new heights.

With partnerships forged and alliances sealed, they stood ready to confront the challenges of cyberspace with unity, solidarity, and unwavering determination.

# 14

# Chapter 14: Data Privacy and Consumer Protection

## 14.1: The Importance of Data Privacy in Banking

Michael Sawyer leaned back in his chair, staring at the wall of monitors in his office. Each screen displayed a different aspect of his bank's operations, from real-time transactions to customer service interactions. Data privacy had become a critical concern, and Michael, as Chief Information Officer, knew that maintaining customer trust hinged on the bank's ability to protect sensitive information.

The morning's meeting had left him uneasy. News of yet another high-profile data breach at a rival bank had sent shockwaves through the industry. As he pondered the implications, his phone buzzed with a call from Rachel Kim, the bank's Chief Privacy Officer.

"Michael, we need to talk," Rachel said urgently. "Can you meet me in the privacy lab in five minutes?"

Michael agreed and made his way to the lab, a secure area where the bank's privacy protocols were developed and tested. Rachel was already there, surrounded by a team of analysts and engineers. She looked up as he entered, her expression serious.

"Michael, our customers' data is our most valuable asset," Rachel began. "If we lose their trust, we lose everything. We need to take immediate action to reinforce our data privacy measures."

Michael nodded, understanding the gravity of the situation. "What do you propose?"

Rachel outlined a comprehensive plan to enhance data privacy. They would implement advanced encryption techniques, bolster access controls, and conduct regular audits to identify and mitigate vulnerabilities. Additionally, they would launch a customer awareness campaign to educate clients about the steps the bank was taking to protect their information.

"We need to be transparent," Rachel emphasized. "Our customers must know that we are committed to safeguarding their data. It's not just about compliance; it's about trust."

The next few weeks were a whirlwind of activity. Michael and Rachel worked closely with their teams, overseeing the implementation of new security protocols and monitoring systems. They also held town hall meetings with employees to emphasize the importance of data privacy and the role everyone played in maintaining it.

One afternoon, Michael received an email from a long-time customer named John. John expressed his concerns about the recent breaches in the industry and sought reassurance that his personal information was safe.

Michael decided to call John personally. "John, I understand your concerns," he began. "I want to assure you that we are doing everything in our power to protect your data. We've implemented new security measures and are continuously working to stay ahead of potential threats."

John was grateful for the personal attention and transparency. "Thank you, Michael. It's good to know that my bank takes this seriously. Trust is everything to me."

As the weeks turned into months, the bank's efforts began to pay off. Customer confidence increased, and they received positive feedback on their commitment to data privacy. Michael and Rachel's proactive approach had not only enhanced security but also strengthened the bond between the bank and its clients.

One evening, as Michael walked out of the office, he felt a sense of accomplishment. The journey was far from over, but they had taken significant steps toward ensuring that their customers' data remained secure. In a world where data breaches and privacy concerns were ever-present, Michael knew that maintaining trust was an ongoing mission—one that required vigilance, innovation, and unwavering dedication.

## 14.2: Regulatory Landscape: GDPR, CCPA, and Beyond

Michael Sawyer's office was buzzing with activity as he prepared for the upcoming meeting with the bank's board of directors. The agenda was dominated by a single, pressing issue: compliance with the evolving regulatory landscape on data privacy. Rachel Kim, the Chief Privacy Officer, had been working tirelessly to ensure the bank's adherence to the General Data Protection Regulation (GDPR), California Consumer Privacy Act (CCPA), and other emerging data protection laws.

As Michael reviewed the latest regulatory updates, he couldn't help but think back to a recent conference in Brussels where he had first truly grasped the global impact of GDPR. The keynote speaker, a leading European data protection officer, had delivered a compelling speech on the importance of safeguarding personal data in an increasingly digital world. The implications were clear: failure to comply could result in hefty fines and, more critically, a loss of customer trust.

Rachel entered the room, carrying a stack of documents. "Ready for this?" she asked, a determined look in her eyes.

"Absolutely," Michael replied. "We've done our homework."

The board meeting began promptly at 10 a.m. Michael and Rachel took their seats at the head of the table, facing a dozen expectant faces. The chairman, Mr. Whitaker, nodded for them to begin.

"Ladies and gentlemen," Michael started, "the regulatory landscape for data privacy is rapidly evolving. Compliance with laws like GDPR and CCPA is not optional; it's a necessity. Today, Rachel and I will outline our strategy to ensure that our bank not only meets but exceeds these requirements."

Rachel took over, presenting a detailed overview of GDPR, which had set the standard for data protection laws worldwide. She explained the stringent requirements for data handling, the rights it granted to consumers, and the heavy penalties for non-compliance. "GDPR is about giving individuals control over their personal data," she emphasized. "It's about transparency, consent, and accountability."

Next, she shifted to CCPA, highlighting its significance for U.S.-based operations. "CCPA provides California residents with similar rights to those under GDPR, including the right to know what personal data is being collected, the right to access that data, and the right to request its deletion. Our compliance with these laws is crucial for maintaining our market presence and customer trust."

The presentation was followed by a barrage of questions from the board members. One director, Mr. Johnson, voiced a common concern: "How are we ensuring that our global operations comply with these diverse regulations?"

Rachel smiled, ready for this. "We've implemented a comprehensive data privacy framework that aligns with both GDPR and CCPA. Our approach includes regular audits, employee training programs, and advanced data management systems. We're also proactive in monitoring and adapting to new regulations as they emerge."

Michael added, "We're not just focused on compliance for the sake of avoiding penalties. Our goal is to build a culture of privacy within our organization. This means embedding privacy principles into every aspect of our operations, from product development to customer service."

The discussion continued for over an hour, covering everything from data breach response plans to the ethical considerations of data usage. By the end, the board members appeared reassured, albeit aware of the challenges ahead.

After the meeting, Michael and Rachel returned to their offices, both feeling the weight of their responsibilities but also a sense of accomplishment. The road to full compliance was arduous, but they were making steady progress.

Later that evening, Michael received an email from an international client expressing gratitude for the bank's transparency regarding data privacy. It was a small victory but a significant one, reaffirming the importance of their efforts.

As Michael shut down his computer for the night, he reflected on the journey ahead. Navigating the regulatory landscape was complex and demanding, but it was also essential for maintaining the integrity and trustworthiness of their bank. With leaders like Rachel by his side, he felt confident that they could meet these challenges head-on, ensuring that their customers' data was protected in an era of unprecedented digital transformation.

## 14.3: Data Governance and Compliance

Michael Sawyer sat in his office, gazing out the window at the cityscape below. It had been a month since the board meeting, and the implementation of their data privacy framework was underway. Yet, he knew that understanding the laws was just the beginning. To truly protect customer data and maintain compliance, they needed a robust data governance strategy.

A knock on his door brought him back to reality. Rachel Kim, the Chief Privacy Officer, walked in with a folder brimming with documents. "Michael, I've outlined our data governance plan," she said, handing him the folder.

Michael opened it and scanned the contents. It was meticulous, detailing every aspect of data management, from collection and storage to access and disposal. "This is impressive, Rachel," he said. "But how do we ensure this is implemented across all departments?"

Rachel smiled. "That's why I scheduled a meeting with our data stewards from each division. They play a crucial role in ensuring that our policies are followed at every level."

The meeting with the data stewards was held in the bank's conference room. Representatives from IT, marketing, finance,

## CHAPTER 14: DATA PRIVACY AND CONSUMER PROTECTION

and customer service gathered around the table, each looking both eager and apprehensive.

"Thank you all for coming," Michael began. "Our goal today is to discuss how we can embed our data governance framework into our daily operations. Compliance is not just an IT issue; it's a responsibility we all share."

Rachel took over, explaining the key components of the data governance framework. "First, we need to establish clear data ownership. Every piece of data must have a designated owner responsible for its integrity and compliance."

She then moved on to data quality. "Accurate and reliable data is essential. We'll implement regular audits and data cleaning processes to ensure that our data remains trustworthy."

Next, Rachel discussed data access controls. "Only authorized personnel should have access to sensitive data. We'll be using role-based access controls to manage who can view and edit specific data sets."

One of the data stewards, Jason from IT, raised a concern. "How do we balance security with usability? We don't want to create bottlenecks that slow down our operations."

Rachel nodded. "It's a delicate balance, but we'll work closely with each department to tailor our controls. The aim is to protect data without hindering productivity."

As the meeting continued, they delved into compliance monitoring. "We'll use automated tools to continuously monitor our data practices," Rachel said. "This will help us detect and address any issues in real-time."

Michael added, "Transparency is key. We need to document all data-related activities and decisions. This not only helps in compliance audits but also builds trust with our customers."

After two hours of intense discussion, the team had a clear

action plan. Each data steward left with specific tasks to implement within their departments.

In the weeks that followed, Michael and Rachel oversaw the rollout of the data governance framework. They encountered challenges—resistance from some employees, technical glitches, and the sheer complexity of managing vast amounts of data. But with persistence and collaboration, they made significant progress.

One day, Michael received an urgent call from Sarah, the head of customer service. "Michael, we've detected a potential data breach. Unauthorized access to customer information."

His heart raced. "I'll be right there."

Michael and Rachel rushed to the incident response room, where a team was already working to contain the breach. Sarah briefed them on the situation: a phishing attack had compromised several employee accounts.

"Activate the breach response plan," Rachel instructed. "Isolate the affected systems and notify the authorities."

As the team worked to mitigate the breach, Michael reflected on the importance of their governance framework. It wasn't just about compliance; it was about being prepared for the unexpected.

After several tense hours, the breach was contained. The damage was limited, thanks to their swift response. Michael addressed the team, "This was a test of our resilience. We handled it well, but we must remain vigilant."

In the aftermath, they conducted a thorough review of the incident, identifying gaps in their defenses and implementing additional safeguards. It was a sobering reminder of the ever-present threats in the digital age.

That evening, Michael returned to his office, exhausted

but determined. He knew that their journey towards robust data governance and compliance was ongoing. It required continuous effort, adaptation, and vigilance. But with leaders like Rachel and the dedication of their team, he was confident they could protect their customers' data and uphold the bank's integrity in an increasingly complex regulatory landscape.

## 14.4: Transparency and Consent Management

Michael Sawyer leaned back in his chair, staring at the latest customer survey results spread across his desk. The feedback was clear: customers wanted more transparency about how their data was being used. They also wanted control over their personal information. It was time to take their data privacy efforts to the next level.

He called Rachel Kim, the Chief Privacy Officer. "Rachel, we need to address transparency and consent management head-on. Can we schedule a meeting with the project team?"

Rachel nodded. "Absolutely. I've been working on some ideas. Let's gather everyone tomorrow morning."

The next day, the team assembled in the innovation lab. A diverse group of professionals from IT, legal, marketing, and customer relations were present, each bringing a unique perspective.

Rachel started the meeting with a presentation. "Our goal is to ensure that our customers understand how their data is being used and give them control over it. We need to implement clear consent management processes."

Michael added, "Transparency isn't just a regulatory requirement. It's a competitive advantage. If we can build trust with our customers, it will differentiate us from our competitors."

Rachel outlined the plan. "First, we need to create a comprehensive privacy dashboard for our customers. This dashboard will allow them to see exactly what data we have, how it's being used, and who it's being shared with."

Jason from IT raised a question. "How do we ensure that the information is presented in a way that is easy for customers to understand?"

"Good point," Rachel said. "We'll need to collaborate with our UX design team. The interface must be user-friendly and informative without being overwhelming."

Samantha from legal chimed in. "We also need to ensure that our consent forms are clear and concise. Customers should be able to grant or withdraw consent for different types of data usage easily."

As they brainstormed, ideas flowed. They decided to use plain language in all communications, avoiding legal jargon that could confuse customers. They would also include visual aids, such as infographics and short videos, to explain complex concepts.

Over the next few weeks, the team worked tirelessly. The UX designers created prototypes of the privacy dashboard, while the IT department built the backend infrastructure to support it. Legal reviewed all the consent forms, ensuring they met regulatory standards while remaining clear and straightforward.

Once the system was ready, they conducted a beta test with a small group of customers. The feedback was overwhelmingly positive. Customers appreciated the transparency and felt empowered by the control they had over their data.

Encouraged by the results, they rolled out the system to all customers. Michael and Rachel closely monitored its impact.

They noticed a significant increase in customer satisfaction scores and a reduction in data-related complaints.

One afternoon, Michael received an email from a long-time customer, Emily Turner. She wrote, "I just wanted to thank you for the new privacy dashboard. For the first time, I feel like I have control over my personal information. It's reassuring to know that my bank values my privacy."

Reading the email, Michael felt a deep sense of accomplishment. This initiative wasn't just about compliance; it was about building trust and respect with their customers.

However, the journey didn't end there. Michael knew that maintaining transparency and managing consent was an ongoing process. They had to stay ahead of regulatory changes and continue to innovate.

He convened a follow-up meeting with the team. "We've made great strides, but we can't become complacent. We need to keep improving our processes and listening to our customers."

Rachel agreed. "We should establish a regular review process for our privacy practices. And let's keep exploring new ways to enhance transparency."

As they wrapped up the meeting, Michael looked around the room, feeling grateful for the dedicated team he had. Together, they had transformed their approach to data privacy, setting a new standard in the banking industry.

In the following months, they continued to refine their privacy dashboard, adding new features based on customer feedback. They also launched educational campaigns to help customers understand the importance of data privacy and their rights.

Through these efforts, Michael realized that transparency

and consent management were not just about meeting regulatory requirements. They were about fostering a culture of trust and respect, one where customers felt valued and secure in their relationship with the bank. This, he knew, was the key to long-term success in the digital age.

## 14.5: Building Trust Through Privacy and Security

Michael Sawyer stood at the front of the auditorium, a place that had come to symbolize the bank's commitment to transparency. This wasn't just a meeting space; it was where they launched initiatives that shaped the future. Today, he was about to unveil their latest project aimed at building trust through enhanced privacy and security measures.

"Ladies and gentlemen," he began, scanning the room filled with colleagues and partners, "our customers have spoken, and we have listened. Trust is the cornerstone of our relationship with them. Today, we're introducing a comprehensive strategy to elevate our privacy and security protocols."

He turned to Rachel Kim, their Chief Privacy Officer, who took the stage with a confident smile. "Our new strategy revolves around three key pillars: transparency, security, and customer empowerment."

Rachel highlighted their efforts to provide clear and accessible information about data usage through the privacy dashboard they had launched recently. "Transparency isn't just about being open; it's about making sure our customers truly understand how their data is being used. We've simplified our privacy policies, integrated visual aids, and offered real-time updates on data usage."

Jason from IT explained the enhanced security measures.

## CHAPTER 14: DATA PRIVACY AND CONSUMER PROTECTION

"We've implemented state-of-the-art encryption and multi-factor authentication across all platforms. Our cybersecurity team is monitoring threats 24/7, ensuring that we stay ahead of potential breaches."

Samantha from legal added, "We're not just focusing on external threats. Internal processes are being revamped to minimize data access points and ensure that only authorized personnel can handle sensitive information."

Michael took the stage again, summarizing the collective effort. "These measures are not just about compliance. They're about respecting our customers' privacy and safeguarding their trust. Let's continue working together to maintain this standard."

After the presentation, Michael and Rachel mingled with attendees, answering questions and gathering feedback. One customer, an elderly woman named Mrs. Roberts, approached Michael.

"Mr. Sawyer," she said, "I've been with this bank for over thirty years. In recent years, I've been worried about my personal information. But with these new measures, I feel much safer."

Her words reaffirmed Michael's belief in the importance of their mission. "Thank you, Mrs. Roberts. Your trust means everything to us, and we're committed to keeping it."

As the days turned into weeks, the impact of their initiatives became evident. Customer satisfaction scores rose, and there was a notable decline in privacy-related complaints. The bank's reputation for prioritizing customer trust spread, attracting new clients who valued security and transparency.

One evening, Michael received a call from Rachel. "I just got off a call with a tech journalist. They're writing a feature on our privacy and security measures. They see us as industry leaders in this area."

"That's great news, Rachel," Michael replied. "But we can't rest on our laurels. We need to keep pushing forward."

Michael knew that trust was fragile. One misstep could undo years of hard work. He gathered his team for a strategy session. "We need to stay vigilant. Cyber threats are constantly evolving, and so must our defenses. Let's brainstorm on how we can further enhance our privacy and security measures."

The team discussed various ideas, from implementing biometric authentication to exploring advanced AI-driven threat detection systems. They also talked about the importance of continuous customer education, ensuring that clients were aware of the latest security practices and how to protect themselves.

As the meeting concluded, Michael felt a renewed sense of purpose. He looked around at his team, a group of dedicated professionals committed to the same goal: building and maintaining customer trust.

In the following months, they launched several new initiatives, including a series of webinars on data privacy and security, interactive tools for customers to manage their data, and partnerships with cybersecurity firms to stay ahead of emerging threats.

Michael also made it a point to regularly meet with customers, listening to their concerns and feedback. He believed that staying connected with the people they served was crucial to maintaining trust.

One afternoon, he received an email from a young entrepreneur named Alex. "I've been hesitant to switch banks, but your commitment to privacy and security convinced me to give you a chance. I look forward to growing my business with a bank that values trust as much as I do."

Reading the email, Michael smiled. Trust wasn't just a buzzword; it was a daily commitment, a promise they made to each customer. And as long as they upheld that promise, he knew they would continue to thrive in the ever-evolving landscape of banking.

## 14.6: Emerging Trends in Data Privacy Regulation

The conference room buzzed with anticipation as the attendees settled into their seats, eager to hear about the latest developments in data privacy regulation. Michael Sawyer, the CEO of the bank, stood at the front of the room, ready to address the crowd.

"Good morning, everyone," Michael began, his voice carrying across the room. "As we navigate the ever-changing landscape of data privacy regulation, it's crucial that we stay informed and proactive in our approach."

He clicked through a series of slides, highlighting the emerging trends in data privacy regulation. "With the rise of digital transformation and increasing concerns about data privacy, governments around the world are enacting stricter regulations to protect consumer data."

Michael discussed the European Union's General Data Protection Regulation (GDPR) and California's Consumer Privacy Act (CCPA), emphasizing their far-reaching implications for businesses operating in those regions. "These regulations are setting new standards for data protection and empowering consumers with greater control over their personal information."

He went on to discuss the growing trend of data localization laws, which require companies to store and process data within the borders of certain countries. "Data localization laws pose significant challenges for multinational companies, requiring them to adapt their data management practices to comply with varying regulatory requirements."

Michael also touched upon the evolving role of regulatory technology (RegTech) in helping banks navigate the complex landscape of data privacy regulation. "RegTech solutions offer automated compliance tools and real-time monitoring capabilities, enabling banks to stay ahead of regulatory changes and streamline their compliance processes."

As the presentation concluded, Michael opened the floor to questions and discussion. The audience engaged eagerly, sharing insights and experiences from their respective organizations.

After the session, Michael received positive feedback from attendees, praising the bank's proactive approach to data privacy regulation. He knew that staying abreast of emerging trends and regulations was essential to maintaining the bank's reputation as a trusted custodian of customer data.

As he made his way back to his office, Michael reflected on the importance of continuous learning and adaptation in the fast-paced world of data privacy regulation. The landscape was constantly evolving, but with the right strategies and technologies in place, the bank would continue to thrive in the digital age while upholding its commitment to protecting customer privacy.

# 15

# Chapter 15: The Road Ahead: Navigating Uncertainty and Embracing Innovation

## 15.1: Reflections on the Banking Evolution

As the sun set on the bustling city skyline, Michael Sawyer found himself in his office, reflecting on the journey that had led them to this pivotal moment in the bank's history. It had been a long and challenging road, marked by moments of triumph and adversity, but through it all, they had remained steadfast in their commitment to innovation and progress.

Michael leaned back in his chair, casting his gaze out the window at the twinkling lights below. Memories flashed through his mind – the early days of his career, the exhilaration of pioneering new technologies, the moments of doubt and uncertainty. But through every twist and turn, one thing had remained constant: change.

He thought back to the evolution of banking, from the days of brick-and-mortar branches to the digital revolution that had reshaped the industry. "The banking landscape has undergone a remarkable transformation," he mused aloud. "We've witnessed the rise of fintech disruptors, the emergence of new business models, and the relentless march of technological innovation."

But amidst the chaos and uncertainty, there had been moments of clarity – moments when the path forward had become clear, when they had glimpsed the possibilities of the future. "We've learned valuable lessons along the way," Michael continued, his voice tinged with nostalgia. "We've learned that agility is key, that we must be willing to adapt and evolve in the face of change. We've learned that customer-centricity is paramount, that we must always put the needs of our clients first. And perhaps most importantly, we've learned that innovation is the lifeblood of progress, that we must embrace new ideas and technologies if we are to stay ahead of the curve."

As he spoke, Michael's thoughts turned to the challenges that lay ahead – the uncertainties of an ever-changing world, the threats posed by cybercrime and regulatory scrutiny, the shifting sands of consumer behavior. But he was undeterred. If anything, the challenges only fueled his determination to succeed.

"We stand at a crossroads," he said, his voice resolute. "The road ahead is fraught with challenges, but it is also brimming with opportunities. We must chart a course that leads us towards innovation, towards progress, towards a future where banking is more than just a transaction – it's an experience, a partnership, a journey."

With that, Michael rose from his chair, a renewed sense of purpose coursing through his veins. The road ahead would be long and uncertain, but he was ready to face whatever challenges came their way. For in the end, he knew that it was not the destination that mattered, but the journey itself – and he was determined to make theirs a journey worth remembering.

## 15.2: Anticipating Future Disruptions

As Michael pondered the future, he couldn't help but feel a sense of excitement mixed with apprehension. The world of banking was on the cusp of yet another revolution, and the challenges ahead were as daunting as they were exhilarating.

Gathering his team in the boardroom, Michael began, "We've come a long way, but we mustn't rest on our laurels. The landscape of finance is evolving rapidly, and we must anticipate the disruptions that lie ahead."

He paced the room, his mind buzzing with ideas and possibilities. "Fintech startups, artificial intelligence, blockchain – these are just the beginning. We must be vigilant, constantly scanning the horizon for new technologies and trends that could reshape the industry."

The team nodded in agreement, their faces reflecting a mixture of determination and concern. They knew that staying ahead of the curve would require relentless vigilance and a willingness to embrace change.

"We must also be mindful of the risks," Michael cautioned. "Cybersecurity threats, regulatory challenges, economic instability – these are just a few of the obstacles we may face. But with careful planning and strategic foresight, we can overcome them."

He looked around the room, meeting each team member's gaze with a steely resolve. "The road ahead will be challenging, but I have no doubt that we have the talent, the expertise, and the determination to succeed. Together, we will navigate the uncertainties of the future and emerge stronger than ever before."

With renewed determination, the team set to work, brainstorming ideas, analyzing trends, and devising strategies to prepare for the disruptions that lay ahead. As they worked late into the night, their spirits were buoyed by the knowledge that they were not facing the challenges alone – they were facing them together, as a team, united in their commitment to shaping the future of banking.

## 15.3: Strategies for Innovation and Adaptation

As the sun rose on a new day, Michael gathered his team once again, this time to discuss the strategies they would employ to innovate and adapt in the face of uncertainty.

"Change is inevitable," Michael began, his voice steady and resolute. "But it's how we respond to that change that defines us. We must be proactive in our approach, constantly seeking out new opportunities for innovation and growth."

He gestured to the whiteboard behind him, where a series of bold ideas and initiatives were outlined in vibrant marker. "These are our strategies for the future – our roadmap for success in the ever-changing world of banking."

The team leaned forward eagerly, their eyes alight with anticipation. They knew that the challenges ahead would be formidable, but they were ready to face them head-on, armed with creativity, determination, and a willingness to think outside the box.

"We must embrace a culture of experimentation," Michael continued, his passion evident in every word. "We must encourage our team members to take risks, to challenge the status quo, to push the boundaries of what's possible. Only then can we truly unleash the full potential of our organization."

He outlined a series of initiatives aimed at fostering innovation, from hackathons and innovation labs to cross-functional collaboration and knowledge sharing. "We must break down silos and cultivate an environment where ideas can flourish – where everyone feels empowered to contribute, regardless of their role or title."

But innovation alone would not be enough. Adaptation was equally crucial, especially in an industry as dynamic and unpredictable as banking. Michael emphasized the importance of agility and flexibility, urging the team to be responsive to changing market conditions and customer needs.

"We must be willing to pivot when necessary," he said. "To pivot quickly and decisively in response to changing circumstances. Whether it's shifting our focus to new markets, redesigning our products and services, or reimagining our business model entirely – we must be willing to adapt and evolve with the times."

As the meeting drew to a close, Michael surveyed the room, a sense of pride swelling within him. He knew that the road ahead would be challenging, but with the right strategies in place and a team of talented individuals by their side, he was confident that they could overcome any obstacle and emerge stronger than ever before.

## 15.4: Investing in Talent and Culture Change

Gathered in the heart of the bank's headquarters, Michael addressed his team, emphasizing the critical importance of investing in talent and fostering a culture of change.

"Talent is our greatest asset," Michael began, his voice carrying a sense of urgency. "In order to thrive in the face of uncertainty, we must attract, develop, and retain the best and brightest minds in the industry."

He spoke passionately about the need to cultivate a diverse and inclusive workforce, one that brought together individuals from a wide range of backgrounds and perspectives. "Diversity drives innovation," he declared. "It sparks creativity, fosters collaboration, and enables us to better serve the needs of our diverse customer base."

But attracting top talent was only the first step. Michael knew that in order to truly succeed, they would need to invest in ongoing learning and development opportunities for their employees. "We must provide our team members with the tools and resources they need to succeed," he said. "Whether it's through formal training programs, mentorship opportunities, or access to cutting-edge technologies – we must empower them to reach their full potential."

But perhaps most importantly, Michael emphasized the need for a cultural shift – a transformation in the way they approached work and innovation. "Culture change is not easy," he admitted. "It requires time, effort, and a commitment from each and every one of us. But if we are to thrive in the new era of banking, it is absolutely essential."

He outlined a series of initiatives aimed at fostering a culture of agility, experimentation, and continuous improvement –

from flexible work arrangements and cross-functional teams to recognition programs and leadership development initiatives. "We must challenge the status quo, question assumptions, and embrace failure as a necessary step on the path to success," he said. "Only then can we truly unleash the full potential of our organization."

As the meeting came to a close, Michael looked out at his team, a sense of optimism coursing through his veins. He knew that the road ahead would be challenging, but with the right investment in talent and a commitment to cultural change, he was confident that they could overcome any obstacle and emerge stronger than ever before.

## 15.5: Collaboration and Ecosystem Building

In the bustling meeting room, Michael stood at the forefront, his gaze fixed on the attentive faces before him. He knew that to navigate the uncertainties of the future, collaboration and ecosystem building were paramount.

"None of us can succeed alone," Michael began, his voice resonating with conviction. "We must forge strategic partnerships and build robust ecosystems that enable us to leverage the strengths of others and amplify our impact."

He gestured to the diagram projected onto the screen behind him, illustrating a network of interconnected organizations, each playing a unique role in the broader ecosystem. "By collaborating with fintech startups, technology providers, regulators, and other industry players, we can drive innovation, accelerate growth, and create value for our customers."

Michael spoke passionately about the power of collaboration – how it could help them access new markets, enter new industries, and unlock new sources of revenue. "Together, we can achieve far more than we ever could alone," he declared. "But collaboration is not just about signing agreements and shaking hands. It's about building trust, fostering transparency, and working towards shared goals."

He outlined a series of initiatives aimed at fostering collaboration within and beyond the organization – from cross-functional task forces and innovation hubs to co-creation workshops and industry alliances. "We must break down the barriers that divide us and embrace a spirit of cooperation," he said. "Only then can we harness the full potential of the ecosystem and chart a course for success in the new era of banking."

As the meeting drew to a close, Michael looked out at the faces before him, a sense of optimism washing over him. He knew that the road ahead would be challenging, but with a commitment to collaboration and ecosystem building, he was confident that they could overcome any obstacle and emerge stronger than ever before.

## 15.6: Charting a Course for Success in the New Era of Banking

In the dimly lit boardroom, Michael stood before his team, the weight of responsibility heavy on his shoulders. This final subpoint was crucial – it encapsulated their collective vision for the future, the culmination of months of planning, strategizing, and soul-searching.

"Charting a course for success in the new era of banking requires boldness, foresight, and unwavering determination," Michael began, his voice steady and resolute. "It's about embracing change, seizing opportunities, and leading with purpose."

He gestured to the map spread out on the table before them, each line and curve representing a potential path forward. "Our journey will be fraught with challenges and uncertainties," he acknowledged. "But if we stay true to our values, remain agile in our approach, and keep our eyes fixed on the horizon, I have no doubt that we will emerge victorious."

Michael spoke passionately about the need to stay ahead of the curve – to anticipate market trends, disrupt conventional thinking, and innovate relentlessly. "We must be pioneers, trailblazers, and visionaries," he declared. "We must challenge the status quo, reimagine the future, and push the boundaries of what's possible."

But success, he knew, was about more than just financial gain. It was about making a positive impact – on their customers, their communities, and the world at large. "We have a responsibility to use our influence for good," he said. "To drive positive change, foster inclusivity, and build a more sustainable, equitable future for all."

As the meeting drew to a close, Michael looked out at his team, a sense of determination burning in his eyes. "The road ahead will not be easy," he admitted. "But with courage, resilience, and a shared sense of purpose, I know that we can overcome any obstacle and achieve greatness together."

And with that, they set forth on their journey, ready to chart a bold new course for success in the ever-evolving landscape of banking.

# About the Author

Goodson Mumba is a multifaceted individual known for his diverse expertise and prolific contributions across various fields. As an infopreneur, Management Consultant, thought leader, and spiritual leader, he has inspired countless individuals through his insightful teachings and impactful writings. Mumba is also an accomplished author, with several notable works to his name, including "Understanding Corporate Worship," "The Years I Spent in a Week," "Management By Harmony," "The CEO's Diary," "Change to Change" and "Creative Thinking for results" His literary works span topics ranging from business management to personal development and spirituality, reflecting his broad range of interests and insights.

With a Master of Business Leadership (MBL) and a Bachelor of Arts in Theology (BTh), Mumba brings a unique blend of business acumen and spiritual wisdom to his work. His educational background is further enriched by a Group Diploma in Management Studies, providing him with a solid foundation in organizational dynamics and leadership principles. Additionally, Mumba holds diplomas in Education Psychology, Leadership and Management Styles, Organizational Behaviour, Financial Accounting, Economic Growth and Development, and Project Management, showcasing his commitment to continuous learning and professional development.

Mumba's expertise extends beyond traditional academic disciplines, encompassing areas such as Neuro-Linguistic Programming (NLP) and Positive Psychology. His diverse skill set is complemented by a range of certifications, including Creative Problem Solving and Decision Making, Life Coaching Fundamentals and Techniques, Professional Life Coaching, and Performance Management System Design. These certifications reflect Mumba's dedication to equipping himself with the tools and knowledge necessary to empower others and drive positive change.

As an author, Mumba's writings reflect his deep understanding of human nature, organizational dynamics, and spiritual principles. His works offer practical insights, actionable strategies, and inspirational guidance for individuals seeking personal growth, professional success, and spiritual fulfillment. Mumba's holistic approach to life and leadership resonates with readers worldwide, making him a respected figure in both the business and spiritual communities.

Overall, Goodson Mumba's diverse background, extensive knowledge, and profound insights make him a sought-after speaker, mentor, and author. His commitment to excellence, lifelong learning, and service to others continues to inspire individuals to unlock their full potential and lead lives of purpose and significance.

Goodson Mumba is renowned for initiating the concept of Management by Harmony, revolutionizing traditional management practices with a focus on balanced and holistic approaches. He has authored two influential books on this subject: "Introduction to Management by Harmony" and its sequel, "Management by Harmony."

Mumba's work has significantly impacted the field, offering innovative strategies for fostering organizational harmony and efficiency. His contributions continue to shape contemporary management theories and practices.

www.ingramcontent.com/pod-product-compliance
Lightning Source LLC
Chambersburg PA
CBHW071827210526
45479CB00001B/30